SERVING WITH CHRIST

A Study of
Jesus' Farewell Commission
to His Disciples

R. Wade Paschal, Jr.

DISCIPLESHIP RESOURCES
MATERIALS FOR GROWTH IN CHRISTIAN FAITH & LIFE
—— NASHVILLE, TENNESSEE ——
P.O. BOX 840 • NASHVILLE, TN 37202 • PHONE (615) 340-7068

Reprinted 1996

Cover design by Graphic Matters.

Library of Congress Catalog Card No. 94-72242

ISBN 0-88177-137-6

DR137

CONTENTS

To My Parents,
Robert and Polly Paschal

PREFACE

As a young Christian in college, I attended a convention along with thousands of other Christian college students in Illinois. I think my major motivation for going was to spend time with my girlfriend. However, the speakers at the convention made a major impact on me. Each morning of the conference started with a Bible study led by the Reverend John Stott, who took us through chapters 13-17 of John. I do not remember much of what he said specifically, but I was deeply moved by his message.

Little did I know then that John 13-17 would be a major concern later in my life. After seminary, I decided to pursue doctoral studies and chose John 17 as the major focus for my dissertation. I began to see that behind the simplicity of the language of the Gospel lay a very complex and serious theology. The Gospel of John challenges the Christian to make a decision for or against Christ. John scorns halfway measures and tentative faith. I began to see that the Gospel was written to encourage people who were being pressured to compromise or even to give up their faith in Christ. In the face of this pressure and even persecution, the Gospel of John calls Christians to stand fast in their commitment and to follow the example of Christ.

This study is by no means intended as a technical discussion of John 13-17. Instead, I have emphasized the pastoral and personal lessons of these chapters. I hope the technical work I have done will help explain some of the more difficult parts of these chapters and make sense of the work as a whole. I have tried to use my scholarly work as a tool to make the chapters understandable and relevant.

I have many people to thank for their help in this work. Of course, my professors, Dr. Ernst Bammel and Professor Christopher Rowland, gave me wonderful guidance in my dissertation. The churches I have served—First United Methodist Church of Tulsa and First United Methodist Church of Ardmore—have taught me even more about what it means to live out the life of faith in Christ. Dr. Craig Gallaway has been a very helpful and encouraging editor and friend. What mistakes are left are entirely my own. As Christ is the example for all of us, I am especially thankful for those who have been examples for me of faith in Christ: John Collier, Tom Albin, L.D. Thomas, Jr., Harriett Thomas, James Buskirk, Darrell Cates, Mike Aldrich, David Seamands, and my wife, Sandi. I am especially thankful for my parents, Robert and Polly Paschal, who made commitment to Christ a living priority in their home and who did not merely talk about sacrificial love, but lived it.

1

THE EXAMPLE OF THE MASTER

Every time I go out to mow the lawn, our two-year-old daughter, Nikola, eagerly follows. At a safe distance she takes a push-toy and carefully mimics everything I do, walking up and down her little bit of lawn as I huff and puff in the Oklahoma heat.

Nikola is eagerly learning everything she can about life from the people around her. She tries to dress like her sister, play with a ball like her brother, and work at the desk like her mother. She is learning by watching what others do and copying them as closely as possible.

Adults learn by copying too. People naturally want to learn from what works. Successful TV shows lead to spinoffs and copycats that try to recreate the "formula." Football coaches eagerly study and duplicate the schemes of last year's champions. We watch what others do and try to copy what seems to accomplish our goals.

Christians do the same. In a study of pastors and how they learn about ministry, clergy indicated that they preferred to learn from other pastors who shared from their own experience. Theoretical presentations from professors ranked fairly low— pastors would rather hear from someone who could speak to their day-to-day needs.[1] We value models and mentors in life, because we find it easier to *see* what to do than simply to learn by hearing.

Jesus seeks to take advantage of this principle in John 13. The disciples want to be like Jesus. They want to perform the miracles he performs, and have the influence and power he has.

Now Jesus is going to show them how. When they are gathered together in the Upper Room, he removes his outer garment, takes a towel and a bowl, and one by one, washes the disciples' feet. The act doubtlessly perplexes the disciples. Like all students, they are looking for a successful model to copy, but washing feet does not seem like a promising road to power and prestige.

As Jesus washes their feet, he is purposefully modeling the hopes and dreams he has for those who will follow him and carry on his ministry. He is giving the disciples a vivid, graphic image to imitate. Jesus washes the feet of the disciples with the cross clearly ahead. The footwashing interprets not only what Jesus has done, but what he is about to do. We may think we already know the point he is making: He wants us to serve! While that is true, service as Jesus serves is not as easy or as simple as it might appear. The act of washing the disciples' feet creates profoundly disturbing and challenging implications for them and for us.

Jesus' Farewell Act

Jesus washes the disciples' feet at the turning point of the book of John. In John 1-12 the action revolves around the question, "Who is Jesus?" However, in John 13-17 the content narrows the focus to the concerns of the disciples. The key question becomes, "How do we live as disciples of Christ, as Jesus leaves us?"

These chapters take the form of what scholars call a "Farewell Discourse." A farewell discourse presents the last sayings of an important figure. These last words summarize the life and purpose of the person in order to instruct the audience.

In our culture, the retirement dinner serves much the same function. A few years ago, a pastor friend of mine retired from a long-time appointment. We all got together for a banquet honoring his splendid ministries. At the end, the pastor stood up and gave the obligatory speech. In the speech, he went through the history of his ministry, citing the highlights of what had happened to the church and to him. He told of his successes as an example of what he hoped we *would* do, and he told of his failures to warn us what *not* to do. He finished by wishing his successor well, and hoping that the good things we had seen begun in the church would continue.

These chapters in John look and sound a good deal like my friend's retirement banquet. Jesus reviews his life and ministry, and he tries to warn the disciples what they will face in the future. He commissions them as his successors and urges them to carry on his ministry.

What does it mean to "carry on" the ministry of Jesus? All through the Gospels, Jesus has attracted people to himself through his miracles and his teachings. In the Gospels we see his disciples trying to emulate him—both successfully (Mk. 6:7-13 and parallels) and unsuccessfully (Mk. 9:14-29). We even see people who evidently remained outside the main group of disciples trying to duplicate his miracles (Lk. 9:49-50). The disciples press forward eagerly to share the glory, and they react jealously if one of them claims too much for himself (Lk. 22:24; Mk. 10:41). Though they are eager to claim the privileges of Jesus' ministry, the disciples do not understand what it will truly mean to carry on that ministry.

John 13:1 suggests that Jesus understood all too well the crisis lying ahead for the small band gathered at the Last Supper:

> Now before the festival of the Passover, Jesus knew that his hour had come to depart from this world and go to the Father. Having loved his own who were in the world, he loved them to the end.

The next few chapters look forward to the critical point of "the hour." Throughout the book of John we have been told to expect "the hour" (see 2:4; 5:28; 7:6f; 12:27). The reference to time tells us that a moment is coming that will provide a climactic resolution to Jesus' life and mission. "The hour" points to a divine destiny that permeates everything Jesus has done. Now the disciples and Jesus stand at this critical juncture, ready to achieve the purposes of God.

In this "hour," however, neither his sense of destiny nor even his obedience to the divine will motivates what Jesus does. As Jesus faces his hour, love moves him toward the cross. Because he loves those who believe in him, he is willing to love them by sacrificing himself for them.

Love, as John understands love, means giving oneself for others. Love naturally leads to action on behalf of the people loved. The cross ultimately speaks most of God's willingness to love—to love at terrible cost and through horrible pain. John 3:16 tells us "God so loved the world that he gave his only Son." In the incarnation and in his ministry, Jesus has been giving of himself in love. Now the self-giving love of the Son will sum itself up in obedience on the cross.

Knowing that the end of his life and ministry has come, and loving his disciples, Jesus wants to do something that will epitomize who he is, what his life means, and what he hopes for the disciples. In that context, Jesus takes the bowl and towel and begins to wash the feet of the disciples.

Peter

In a day when most streets were dirt streets, and when most sanitation, where it existed at all, meant an open sewer running down the street, washing the feet of a guest was a practical bit of hospitality. The familiar Leonardo da Vinci painting of the disciples sitting around the table does not reflect first-century habits. Most likely, the disciples and Jesus lay on the floor and ate off a very low table, reclining on one arm and eating with the other.

The feet of one person would recline behind the head of another. Later, the beloved disciple is described as reclining by the breast of Jesus (13:23), suggesting that he was lying on the floor next to Jesus, with his head near Jesus' chest.

Reclining around the table in this way, we can imagine why one needed someone to wash the feet of one's neighbors! The meal would no doubt taste much better if the dust and the muck of the day's journey were washed from your fellow diners.

Normally, a servant or a younger child of the host family would perform this task. Washing the feet of a guest was a messy and smelly job. In the absence of a servant or a child, the eldest would normally delegate the task to the youngest person or the one with the least status among the group. It was up to the disciples to have someone from among themselves perform the footwashing. No one wanted to volunteer. Apart from the distasteful nature of the task, who wanted to admit to being the lowest of the twelve?

When Jesus takes up the towel and the bowl and washes the feet of the disciples, he overturns the natural order of things. He has the title of "teacher" and "master," but he serves those who should be serving him. He does not demand his rights but gives to others what he could claim.

Of course, Jesus has been reversing expectations through-out his ministry. In John 2 he overturned the tables of the moneychangers at the temple as an act of prophetic judgment against "religion as usual." Then in John 4 Jesus talked with and accepted the scandalous woman of Samaria. In John 9 he touched and healed the man born blind, whom the rulers of the temple scorned as one "born entirely in sins" (v. 34). The foot-washing provides an interpretation for all these events where Jesus inverts the natural order: Jesus has come to care for and to serve the lowliest of people and their common needs, and to reject privilege and status.

The footwashing not only interprets Jesus' past, but also looks ahead to his future acts. The washing of the disciples' feet points toward the cross. John sees the cross as the essence of love. Jesus always intended to die for others so that they could find life and resurrection. In washing the disciples' feet, Jesus acts out a dramatic metaphor for the cross: love which meets the unpalatable needs of the beloved.

As we might expect, Peter has trouble understanding what Jesus is doing. Peter does not want Jesus to jump out of his expected role. Jesus should remain as "Master," which means getting one's feet washed, not doing the washing. Peter has no desire for Jesus to serve him!

Why does Peter try to refuse Jesus' act of service? The Gospel writer does not try to analyze Peter's motives, but refusing Jesus had serious implications. Jesus responds with some tough words for Peter, "Unless I wash you, you have no share with me" (13:8). Peter cannot refuse Jesus' service without refusing Jesus himself. Accepting Christ and being part of his kingdom means accepting the service of Christ and our need for that service.

We can imagine why we would find it hard to let Jesus wash our feet. Receiving help often feels awkward. Anyone who has visited a friend in the hospital (or had to stay personally overnight) has observed the discomfort most of us feel when forced into a position of receiving care. We do not like feeling helpless. We fight against being out of control. We may even feel guilty when forced to receive help, as if we were not quite all right.

This suggests why our resistance to being served must be overcome: To be Jesus' disciples, we must admit that we are not quite all right and that we need help. We need a savior. Apart from Christ's death for us, we could not find forgiveness or eternal life. We need help, and we may find admitting that need difficult. Peter's hesitancy to receive Jesus' service may reflect the discomfort we all feel when put in the position of receiving.

It could be, too, that the image of a humble Jesus serving his followers offended Peter's pride and personal hopes for glory.

If Jesus takes up the towel and the bowl, what does that imply for his followers? What glory or privilege is it to follow a leader who washes feet? In rejecting Jesus' act of service, it may be that Peter is refusing to lower himself. To affirm Jesus' humble service Peter realizes he must deny his own desire for power and privilege, so he resists.

If Peter wants to be like Jesus, however, he must reckon with this humility. When Jesus washes the disciples' feet, he is again acting out his essential nature. Laying aside his rights and status for the needs of others defines Jesus' fundamental self-concept. Long before the footwashing, Jesus had already profoundly lowered himself. As John has already told us, in Jesus the "Word became flesh" (Jn. 1:14), and left his "glory" for the sake of others (Jn. 17:5). In this sense, Jesus is not asking Peter to do anything that he has not already done. In John 11, Mary washed his feet. If Luke 7:36-50 represents a separate incident, Jesus was even willing to receive help from a woman of doubtful reputation. The humility Christ was looking for in Peter was the same humility he had already demonstrated in his own life. This suggests that the order here is intentional: To follow Christ means learning to receive before we attempt to serve.

Jesus has good reason for insisting that Peter learn to receive. On the one hand, receiving service will help Peter escape the temptation to develop an arrogant and condescending spirit in his future service. Sometimes service and charity can emphasize the distance between people. However, Jesus sacrifices himself for others without ever implying that he is a superior being sacrificing himself for inferior and needy people. Jesus touched, healed, and helped the poor, the sick, and the outcast without ever demeaning them because of their need. Instead, he identified with them and lifted them up as he ministered to them. The footwashing suggests to us that all of us must receive; therefore none of us can see our service as anything but an act of gratitude and love in response to what we have been given.

However, Jesus is concerned with more than just making sure Peter will be a good and humble servant. Without receiving service, Peter can have no "share with" Jesus. Being a disciple always means trusting in and relying on God. We never reach a time when we have strength in ourselves. Our strength always comes in relationship with Christ. Part of being a Christian means being on the receiving end of God's grace and God's love. Until Peter understands this, he cannot truly follow Christ.

Peter, being Peter, cannot leave well enough alone. Having been rebuked for refusing to allow Jesus to wash his feet, he now asks Jesus to wash his whole body. In any event, we are reminded of our own pride and self-centeredness. It is as if Peter thinks, "Well, if I'm going to have Jesus wash me, I'm going to have more washed and be better washed than anyone else." Peter seems to resist being treated like all the rest. He appears worried about his status. He wants to be set apart as different, even in the gracious giving of his Lord.

Jesus quickly calls Peter back to the point. He tells him, "One who has bathed does not need to wash, except for the feet, but is entirely clean" (Jn. 13:10). The need to be special, to be singled out and lifted above the masses, simply betrays our pride and our entrapment in the old order. In fact, all of us have to be "cleansed" through God's grace and love. None of us needs this more than another. All people are equally needy before God.

The simple act of receiving service strips away the pretense of self-sufficiency. If you are on the receiving end of service, you have given up control and allowed another person to be in the superior position. This vulnerability makes us extremely uncomfortable. We often resist being served precisely because of the implication that we need someone or something beyond ourselves; however, this vulnerability and self-forgetfulness again lie at the heart of Jesus' person and mission. Being like Jesus means laying aside the need to be different or to stand above the crowd. We can only serve like Jesus when we have let go of the need to control and save ourselves.

Throughout these verses, Peter serves as a contrast to Jesus. Peter is proud; Jesus is humble. Peter draws attention to himself; Jesus draws attention to the needs of others. Peter wants control; Jesus gives up control. Peter is fearful and suspicious of giving himself; Jesus gives himself freely. The depth and breadth of Jesus' service are laid out before us. If we ever have a tendency to use the words *service* and *love* lightly, this scene should make us pause. As Jesus washes the disciples' feet, we are seeing a humility and self-forgetfulness that go far beyond doing a good deed. The love modeled here knows how to give and how to receive, and how to serve without subtly manipulating people to give back in return.

The Betrayer

Jesus' final words to Peter, "And you are clean, though not all of you," suggest another issue. Note John's explanation of this phrase: "For he knew who was to betray him; for this reason he said, 'Not all of you are clean' " (Jn. 13:11).

Along with all the rest of the disciples, Jesus also washed the feet of Judas. He knew that Judas would betray him, yet he washed his feet. Jesus was willing to serve and to love even the one who rejected him. Jesus served not only undeserving people, but also those who were hostile and angry.

We tend to dole out our service and charity carefully. We fear giving to the undeserving. This may in part reflect a sensible desire to make good use of our resources. However, at another level, the conditional nature of our giving sometimes reflects our discomfort with giving at all. People on the receiving end of service and charity sometimes feel more judgment than grace from those doing the giving.

George Bernard Shaw lampoons the condemning nature that he felt undercut so-called Christian charity in his play *Pygmalion*, through the character of Alfred Doolittle:

> What am I, Governors…? I ask you, what am I? I'm one of the undeserving poor; that's what I am. Think of what that means to a man. It means that he's up again' middle class morality all the time. If there's anything going, and I put in for a bit of it, it's always the same story: "You're undeserving; so you cant have it." But my needs is as great as the most deserving widow's that ever got money out of six different charities in one week for the death of the same husband. I don't need less than a deserving man: I need more. I don't eat less hearty than him; and I drink a lot more. . . . Well, they charge me just the same for everything as they charge the deserving. What is middle class morality? Just an excuse for never giving me anything.[2]

Doolittle represents the giving person's worst nightmare—the person who wants help without responsibility, charity that in no way makes him better. In view of such a character, how easy it is to put restraints and conditions on giving! We naturally want people to justify our giving through their response.

Jesus' treatment of Judas flies in the face of this. Jesus knew that Judas would fail him, yet Jesus washed his feet anyway. This becomes the true measure of service—giving irrespective of the response of the person receiving the service. Next to Jesus' washing the feet of Judas, much of our service seems manipulative and proud. We begin to believe we are doing others a favor by serving them, and we expect them to show proper appreciation. We give to others, and we expect a sort of servile gratitude as our pay in return.

There may be no harder point for any of us than to love and to serve those who reject us. We have a natural tendency to avoid difficult people. If someone rejects us, we simply want to move on and work with those who respond positively. Why waste time on those who not only lack appreciation for what we do, but curse us for it?

Jesus, nevertheless, does not live this way. Just as he washes the feet of his betrayer, he also dies for those who will hate and abuse him. Love does not pick or choose people for its own comfort. The fact that one of his own disciples betrays him does not stop his determination to serve. His love acts regardless of the response in the heart of the person he is serving.

Does this mean that the response of the person being served makes no difference at all? Jesus deeply wants to reach the disciples and teach them through his service, but he knows not all will respond. His giving has a purpose, but not a demand. He gives, hoping and seeking to affect the twelve. He gives freely to all, trusting that they will freely respond.

In one sense, washing Judas' feet gives us the final step of Jesus' attitude toward serving. Jesus is willing to receive service, because he has no need to control. He knows how to celebrate and to cherish the joy of giving and receiving. Jesus is willing to serve, because he has no false sense of self-importance or need for power. Jesus is willing to serve Judas, because he does not need others to respond in kind to him. We speak of unconditional love, and Jesus shows us what it means. Serving in love, as Jesus serves, means humbling oneself in love for the needs of others without respect to status or prerogatives and without conditions on response or attitudes.

Jesus the Model

Having laid the groundwork through his own act and through his conversation with Peter, Jesus now proceeds to explain the meaning of what he has done:

> *So if I, your Lord and Teacher, have washed your feet,*
> *you also ought to wash one another's feet. For I have set*
> *you an example, that you also should do as I have done*
> *to you (Jn.13:14-15).*

Jesus washed their feet, not only to show them the essence of who he was, but also the essence of who they were to become.

Significantly, Jesus does not divorce his servant action from his actual self. He does not dismiss his real authority and power. Jesus serves because he truly is "Teacher" and "Lord." These positions do not imply privilege for Jesus, but rather the opposite. His "lordship" can only be expressed in service, and the same is true for us.

In a similar passage in Luke 22, Jesus tells the disciples:

> *The kings of the Gentiles lord it over them; and those in*
> *authority over them are called benefactors. But not so*
> *with you; rather the greatest among you must become*
> *like the youngest, and the leader like one who serves*
> *(Lk.22:25-26).*

The kingdom of God reverses the normal human hierarchy where the greater are served by the lesser. For Jesus, greatness means service. It is not simply that the great ought to serve, but that spiritual leadership and power can only be achieved in service. Moreover, the true goals of the spiritual life—love, joy, and hope—can only be achieved in this way.

If Jesus expressed his lordship in service, how much more do we who follow Jesus need to do the same. Human nature loves ease and comfort. One of the beneficial results of having gifts and power comes in the form of prerogatives. How easily the church falls in step with the world, giving special honor and privileges to those who are given leadership roles or who have unusual talents or possessions.

While working in a downtown church, we on staff used to take turns dealing with the requests from transients and street people who would come to the door seeking help. The minister detailed to work with these requests was called "The Minister of the Day," or more prosaically, "MOD." None of us relished the task. We were tempted to view "Minister of the Day" duty as a nuisance that kept us away from the specialized tasks for which we were trained as educators, evangelists, and counselors.

I suspect that some of our reluctance in handling the MOD calls lay in the helplessness we all felt in dealing with those needy and troubled people. The people who came to us were not easy to help. Some were dealing with obvious alcohol or drug problems. We could smell on their breath where their last dollar had gone. Frequently we heard stories we knew could not be true.

Our ability to help these folks seemed tragically limited. We would see people who were horribly ill-equipped to deal with the demands of the modern world, either through lack of education or poor family situations. They needed jobs and money but had few personal tools to get either. Others were just out of a mental institution, dumped on the street long before they were really healthy and ready to live on their own. We might help them, but we could not cure them.

The problems we saw were deep and complex. We helped with food, clothing, and housing, but these seemed like mere bandages that we slapped on horrible wounds. Few wanted more help than that, even when we had resources. Most were too hurt to believe they could be healed or helped. For proud, professional ministers who were constantly praised in their normal area of expertise for their ability to "do things," the frustration of being able to do so little gnawed at every one of us.

In some ways my days as MOD were among the most profound of all my ministry. By this, I do not mean that I saw some miraculous turnabouts for people. While we did help some, the more substantive miracles occurred in me. My MOD clients helped me admit how narrow and shallow were my own abilities to help, especially compared to how deep some hurts and needs went. I also had to admit how proud much of my "ministry" was. I enjoyed being recognized for how well I did my job. At times I gave lip service to Christ, while greedily lapping up the glory that came my way.

My days as MOD taught me to do what I could and to trust God. Contact with the least lovely of people made me realize the greatness of divine love in God's acceptance of the least lovely parts of my own life. I was reminded over and over again that God did not give up on me, and I was not allowed to give up on others. Though I could not solve all their problems, God's grace gave me freedom to do what good I could.

I often struggled to respect the unwashed and drunken people who came to us, but this very struggle revealed to me how far I had to go in dealing with my false pride and comfortable self-satisfaction. My MOD days rubbed my nose in the weakness of the human flesh and in my weaknesses, too. Step by step, I began to learn how to trust in the grace of God, to enjoy what God in Christ had given to me, and to pass on that grace to others.

Jesus told his disciples, "Very truly, I tell you, servants are not greater than their master, nor are messengers greater than the one who sent them. If you know these things, you are blessed if you do them" (Jn.13:16-17).

At all times, but especially during the Lenten season, Christians take time to contemplate the content and cost of their discipleship. Jesus' action of washing the disciples' feet reminds us what true Christian service requires. Service does not simply mean good deeds. Service, as Christ models it, means touching the dirty and unpleasant parts of people's lives. Service means giving up the pretense that we do not need to be served, as well as giving up the sense of superiority that we are somehow better than others because we serve. We serve because God served us in Christ. Service means being free to serve with Christ.

◉ *Discussion Questions*

1. Read Philippians 2:1-18. How does this passage remind you of John 13? Can you think of other passages in the New or Old Testament that speak of serving in this way?

2. Read Luke 10:25-37, the story of the "good Samaritan." Why did Jesus choose a Samaritan—a person considered "lower class" in first-century Jewish society—to illustrate the nature of true serving and being served?

3. Which is more difficult for you—to serve or to be served? To serve the unlovely or to allow the unlovely to serve you? Why?

4. Write down an example of ministry to others that you feel was truly in the Spirit of Christ. This can be from your own experience or from the experience of someone you know. What makes this example particularly memorable to you?

5. Now think of one action or attitude that you might practice during the coming week in order to serve with Christ. Think of someone or something that needs your service, whether or not you want to serve. Covenant with the Lord, in the power of his Spirit, to serve with him in this way.

2
HUMAN FAILURE AND DIVINE SUCCESS

John and June Jones (not their real names) were leaving town. The Joneses had been very active in their church; they were involved in many ministries, and we were going to miss them greatly. A great business opportunity had opened up in another city, and we wished the Joneses well as they left, hoping for their success.

A year later, quite by accident, I found that John and June had moved back into our city. Virtually none of their friends at the church knew. The great business opportunity had turned out to be a bust, so they had come back in desperate circumstances; however, they had not allowed any of us to know.

No one knows what motivated the Joneses to avoid contact with their former friends and church. Perhaps they felt we had forgotten them as soon as they moved away. Maybe they were too involved with us before and were afraid to renew relationships with us because it would be hard to say "no" to all their former ministries. But, perhaps part of their decision reflected the difficulty we all have with failure. Having left with high hopes and expectations, they must have found it difficult to come home with nothing. Perhaps our exceptionally high opinion of them made it difficult for the Joneses to come back when things were not well.

Failure rattles our self-confidence and undermines our self-image. It makes us feel that we can do nothing. To adapt another saying, failure makes cowards of us all. After a failure, we hesitate to risk. Having failed, we wonder what we have to offer.

On the other hand, the gospel presents the *triumph* of failure.

The sign of our faith—the cross—has become a favorite piece of jewelry. We forget that Roman criminal justice reserved the cross for the worst of all criminals from the lowest social strata. Only bandits, terrorists, and slaves suffered the cruelty and humiliation of crucifixion. As Paul notes, the cross represented failure and presented problems for early Christians: "We proclaim Christ crucified, a stumbling block to Jews and foolishness to Gentiles" (1 Cor. 1:23).

As we begin the second week of our study, John 13 raises many questions about the nature and purpose of Jesus' death. If Jesus was the Word incarnate, why did he not prevent Judas' betrayal? If God is present in Christ, why did he die in such a fashion? How can the church promise eternal life if its leader died? If Jesus was overcome by human forces, how can the church overcome the human opposition it faces?

Although these questions seriously challenged Christian faith, John, like Paul, does not back away from the reality of Jesus' death or from the role of Judas and the rest of the disciples in it. Far from being embarrassed by the death of Jesus, John proclaims the cross as the *triumph* of the Son of God. The tragic chain of events that seems to start in the Upper Room only appears to lead to failure and tragedy.

The Betrayer

All four Gospels agree that Jesus knew his betrayer was among the twelve (Mt. 26:21-25; Mk.14:18-21; Lk. 22:21-23; Jn. 13:21-26). Matthew and John make it clear that Jesus knew Judas was the betrayer. Each Gospel wrestles with the same problem: How could the miracle worker and prophet-Messiah fail to prevent the presence of evil among his closest disciples? If Jesus chose the twelve, why would he choose one who would go so wrong? Was this a sign of weakness in Jesus or an indication of some limitation in him?

The Gospel of John pays particular attention to Judas. In 13:11 the evangelist carefully underlines the fact that Jesus knew one of the twelve was to betray him—that not all of the disciples were "clean." Jesus, therefore, knew and anticipated the work of the betrayer. The inner core of the disciples was chosen with the clear knowledge that one of them would turn against his Master. The reason for this was clear to the Gospel writers. Scripture had foreshadowed it: "It is to fulfill the scripture, 'The one who ate my bread has lifted his heel against me' " (Ps. 41:9).

In one sense, the Gospel writer needs no further reason than this: The betrayal is part of the divine plan that has been unfolding since the beginning of time. Judas' role was part of this pattern just as much as Jesus' birth, ministry, and death.

At this point, however, we need to think clearly and deeply. In our "modern scientific age," we have sometimes tended to think of the fulfillment of scripture in simplistic terms. Does Jesus' statement in John 13:18 imply that Judas was doomed to commit evil by a divine decree? Was Judas merely an innocent dupe, picked upon by divine providence to fulfill unwittingly an obscure prophecy? If so, what would that prove?

On closer examination, John's account of Judas' betrayal appears to operate at a much more dynamic level of meaning and insight. Indeed, John develops a much more complex view of Judas. For one thing, we are told that Judas has an inclination to pilfer from the common treasury (12:6), implying that he has already been seduced by his love of money. At a human level, this love of money leads Judas to betray his master. At the same time, John's reference to Psalm 41:9 places Judas' deceit in the context of the betrayal of grace that we find in every age. Directed as it is against the pure, self-giving love of Jesus, this betrayal becomes the climax and archetype of all human ingratitude and evil.

In this way, John finds multiple layers of meaning in Judas' deed. Greed may directly motivate Judas to betray Jesus, but the moment he begins the betrayal, Judas becomes the tool of cosmic forces greater than himself. When he accepts the piece of bread from Jesus (13:27), Judas becomes the extension of Satan's will and desire.

The betrayal reflects the Gospel's piercing analysis of the reality and power of evil. The betrayal inverts the message of the cross. Judas seeks to sacrifice Jesus for his own needs and lusts. Evil entices us, promising that it is right for us to use and manipulate others for our own needs. We have already met this attitude in Caiaphas, who was ready to sacrifice Jesus to save the country (Jn. 11:51). Judas and Caiaphas illustrate individually the nature of the evil spirit of selfishness and deceit.

The offer of forgiveness and love extended by Jesus offends this spirit of selfishness. Christ empowers an other-centered approach to life that contradicts the power of Satan. Therefore, evil will try anything to attack and obliterate good. The betrayal does not represent merely Judas' greed and failure, but the collaboration of human and spiritual forces to reject God and God's goodness throughout history and time.

At the deepest level, therefore, John sees Judas' personal motivation as part of a much larger pattern. His betrayal participates in the more basic betrayal of God by the creatures of God. Our desire for our own way and our will against the will of God lead us to attack the good that God sends into the world.

In keeping with this, Judas does not provide the only example of failure in the betrayal scene. Even with Jesus' words and actions, the disciples fail to realize that he has pointed out the betrayer to them. They guess that Judas leaves the room for some benign purpose or to make provision for those who are poor (Jn.13:29). They fail to make any move to stop or to challenge the betrayer, because they fail to understand what is happening.

The blindness of the disciples portrays the triumph of evil through human ignorance. Evil not only works actively to attack good, but it also works subtly through inattention and sloth. We participate in evil passively as we stand by and fail to comprehend the significance of the actions in front of us.

After World War II, residents of the nearby German towns were taken to the concentration camps. Over and over the people would say, "We did not know." Given the size of the camps and the stench produced by their grisly operations, this seemed incomprehensible to the soldiers who liberated the camps. Of course, the people could have known had they wished to, but they did not *want* to know. They shut their eyes and noses to the evidence, because they preferred to remain ignorant.

While such enormous horrors may not lie close at hand, most of us have developed the ability not to see what might be uncomfortable. We miss the pain our child or spouse feels when we make a thoughtless comment. We pass by the hurts of people in our own city or social circles. Ignorance sometimes perpetuates or gives permission to evil. Just as the disciples allowed Judas to pass untouched into the night to betray Jesus, we allow many hurts to go on unhindered and unnoticed.

As Judas departs, the Gospel notes simply, "it was *night*." In the betrayal plot, the forces of darkness reach the zenith of their power. It seems that Satan is triumphing. The good that God intends is going to be crucified with Jesus. Human greed and cosmic malice are combining to threaten God's ultimate work in Christ. The darkness of the night mirrors the grim deceit and human arrogance at work in the acts of the betrayer.

The Glory

In this context, the next few verses sound all the more ironic:

When he had gone out, Jesus said, "Now the Son of Man has been glorified, and God has been glorified in him. If God has been glorified in him, God will also glorify him in himself and will glorify him at once" (John 13:31-32).

How can Jesus speak of "glorifying" anything in this context? The act of betrayal seems as far from "glorifying" God or Christ as one could possibly get. The betrayal is an act of dishonor that seems to denote the triumph of evil over God. Yet these verses stress that it is only *after* Judas departs that Jesus says "*now*" is the time of glory.

What could Jesus possibly mean? In one sense, the betrayal will inadvertently reveal the honor of Christ and God. Jesus' death on the cross was an act of obedience and, therefore, is praiseworthy. The Son came with the intention of going to the cross in obedience to God (Jn.12:27-28). Honor belongs to the servant who faithfully carries out his mission.

These verses also reflect the knowledge that God will raise the Son from the dead, showing the faithfulness of God. Therefore, Father and Son both find honor in the cross through their faithful fulfillment of their promises to one another. The Son honors the Father with his obedience in going to the cross, and the Father honors the Son in raising him from the dead.

However, the cross also reveals the "glory" of God in another sense. The use of the title "Son of Man" in these verses signals that a deeper revelation of Christ's nature is at hand. Elsewhere in the Gospel of John, this title typically refers to the heavenly character of Jesus. In 1:51, Jesus speaks of angels ascending and descending upon the "Son of Man." In 3:13-14, Jesus looks forward to the cross and tells us that when he is "lifted up" (through crucifixion) the "Son of Man" will return to heaven, his original home. In 5:27, we read that the "Son of Man" will sit in judgment, and in 6:62 that the "Son of Man" will ascend into heaven.

In short, the Gospel of John uses the "Son of Man" title for Jesus when the emphasis is being placed on his heavenly origin or destiny. The irony again must be intentional: When Jesus seems weakest and most human, God uses this to reveal the Son's divinity and glory.

How can the betrayal lead to "glorification" of God and Christ? It is God's nature to transform darkness into light, death into life, and injustice into justice. The power of the cross lies in its power to transform death and defeat into life and victory. The darkest of all deeds—the betrayal of the Son of God—becomes the doorway to glory, because it leads to light and life for many. The cross and the resurrection transform the betrayal from the triumph of darkness to the triumph of glory.

John's connection between the dark into which the betrayer departs and the revelation of the glory of the Son of Man makes this momentous point: No human circumstance lies beyond the power of God to touch and transform. Although the betrayer escapes into darkness, the promise at the beginning of the Gospel of John is finally being fulfilled: *"The light shines in the darkness and the darkness did not overcome it"* (Jn.1:5).

This is not to say that evil is not real. The cross was real, and the betrayal was real. John does not deny the actual existence of hurt, pain, deceit, and sin; but the resurrection overcomes and transforms evil. In the hands of God, an instrument of torture and shame becomes a sign of God's own power and glory. In the hands of God, human beings, with their own failures and shame, become instruments that further reveal the glory of God.

Church history is thickly populated with saints who have moved from failure to faithfulness. Paul frequently marveled that one who persecuted the church could be used to spread the good news (Gal. 1:13; 1 Cor. 15:9). St. Augustine was deeply involved in self-indulgence and degradation before beginning his ministry. Modern-day people, such as Templeton Award-winner Charles Colson, have made major mistakes in life, yet have gone on to serve God. The resurrecting God takes people in the midst of the worst types of failure and transforms their lives into vehicles of glory.

The lives of those who believe in Christ reveal the glory of God. As Jesus points out to the disciples (Jn.13:31-33), with the resurrection and the ascension, he will no longer be present physically on the earth. If others are to continue to see the glory of God revealed in Christ, it must be through the disciples (Jn.13:35). When people see a difference in the way Christians live, they will more easily be able to believe in the One whom Christians proclaim.

Significantly, at this point Jesus encapsulates all his commandments into one: "... *love one another as I have loved you*" (Jn.15:12). The Gospel of John lacks the extensive ethical teachings we find in Matthew and Luke (especially in the Sermon on the Mount). For John, Jesus has only two commandments: to believe in him and to love one another as he has loved them. Love defines the changed nature of the Christian. This quality above all will convince others that something real happens through faith in Christ.

Jesus calls this a "new" commandment, although the Old Testament already commanded people to love God and to love their neighbor (see Mk. 12:28-34). What is new is not the commandment to love, but the qualifier, "as I have loved you." Jesus loved to the point of death on the cross. Jesus loved the disciples before they understood his love—and he loved them in the midst of their failure.

We sometimes use the term "unconditional love" as if it were a simple and obvious concept. The commandment to love in the context of the betrayal reminds us of the pain and cost of love such as this. We think of love in terms of those who care equally for us and who make our lives a joy. Jesus' love went out to those who rejected and abused him. Jesus' love meant pain, suffering, and death. This love sacrifices all, regardless of whether anyone deserves it.

In his book on the Christian revival that took place among soldiers captured by the Japanese in the Valley of the River Kwai, Ernest Gordon tells a remarkable story.[3] At the end of a day of work, the tools were counted, and a Japanese guard began to insist that one shovel was missing. The guard demanded that the tool be returned and that the thief step forward. When no one moved, the guard began to rant and rave and threaten. "All die, all die!" he shrieked and readied his rifle to fire at the group of POWs.

At that point a young Scottish soldier stepped forward and said, "I did it." The guard began to beat the soldier who made no sound or response. This only angered the guard more, and he increased his fury, finally slamming the butt of his gun into the head of the prisoner. The young Scotsman slumped to the ground and died.

The other prisoners picked up their friend's body and took him back to the camp, along with their tools. Once back they recounted the tools. None were missing.

Remarkably, as Gordon tells it, the prisoners of the camp reacted more with admiration for the young soldier than with hatred for the guard. For them, it was a fulfillment of the command of Jesus, "Love one another as I have loved you." The ability of some to rise above the desperate brutality of the camp and to give themselves to help others became a proof that God had not deserted the prisoners.

Costly love such as that prompts the question: What would enable a person to give sacrificially for others? When we can say, "Because Christ has loved me, I love you," we will truly draw people to Christ.

The Denial

The prediction of Judas' betrayal of Jesus and the prediction of Peter's denial of Jesus stand virtually side by side in every Gospel (see Mt. 26:21-25, 30-35 and the parallel passages in Mark and Luke). Judas and Peter are joined together as twin examples of human failure. While Judas' betrayal ranks as the darker deed, Peter's weaknesses remind us that all of the disciples fail Jesus in varying degrees. Peter ranks first among the disciples, and his denial reminds us of our many all-too-human failings.

John, of all the Gospels, presents Peter's denial in the most dramatic form. In 18:15-27, John paints the portrait of a weak, fearful, and vacillating Peter around the presentation of Jesus during the trial at the house of the high priest. Jesus is strong, bold, and truthful. Peter evades and dodges the truth. The strength of Jesus' commitment to obey the Father and to go to the cross contrasts strongly with the weakness of Peter's commitment to Christ. In John 13:37, Peter boldly states to Jesus, "I will lay down my life for you." Peter will eventually fulfill his promise (Jn.21:19), but he does not yet know how costly and difficult that giving of himself will be. Before he lives up to his bold words and intentions, he will fail.

On the one hand, Peter's example warns us against blithely assuming that we are ready to serve with Christ. We have good intentions, but when we face the cost of our intentions, we may hesitate and falter—or even fail. We earnestly want, and even believe, that we are ready to do great things for God. For most of us, however, failure and mistakes fill the road to realizing our best intentions and commitments.

It is easy to say, "We love Christ and are ready to serve him!" but it is also easy to fall short in our actions. We speak sincerely, but words cost little. Our fears, our selfishness, or our ignorance may shortcut our desire to give of ourselves.

On the other hand, Peter's denial reminds us of a second and greater truth: After Peter denied Jesus, he went on to become the disciple who led the church and who truly did give his life for his faith. One failure, or even many failures, do not mean that we are ruined for service forever.

Peter's experience reminds us that our claims to strength and courage at times ring hollow and false. On our own, we will fall far short of our bravado and self-confidence. However, by realizing our weaknesses and by honestly facing our failures, we are transformed into fit servants of God. Understanding our frailty, we stand at the threshold of being strong in Christ. When we know our brokenness, we can understand the need to point others toward the one who makes us whole.

The servant of Christ does not serve when he or she becomes perfect. The servant of Christ begins service in the midst of personal insufficiency and brokenness. When we deny our failures, we have trouble truly serving God. When we repent of our failures, God can truly use us. As Paul says, "We have this treasure in clay jars, so that it may be made clear that this extraordinary power belongs to God and does not come from us" (2 Cor. 4:7).

In the end, God uses unlikely and flawed people to reach others. Indeed, against the backdrop of human flaws, the brightness of God's glory shines all the more clearly. The frailty of the servants of God becomes the means through which the power and love of God more potently express themselves. We are so clearly ordinary that something extraordinary must motivate us to serve and love others. We love because God first loved us. Nothing else could make us act and be so different from our normal selves.

John Wesley certainly possessed both strengths and weaknesses. He had times of real failure—notably his flawed attempt at mission work in Georgia. Wesley made some dubious decisions in his life, such as his decision to marry Mary Vazeille, who proved to be unable to handle John's itinerate life and the numerous people involved in it. Wesley was often criticized by his opponents for being autocratic; certainly there was nothing democratic about Wesley's administration of the Methodist movement. Most accounts of Wesley paint a portrait of a complex man of strengths and weaknesses, courage and contrariness—a man who deeply affected many for the good, yet infuriated others.

Despite his lifelong preaching of perfection and his own robust self-confidence, Wesley also had his moments of doubt and self-criticism. In one letter to his brother in 1766, Wesley called himself, "[an] honest heathen, a proselyte of the Temple" and claims that he never "*believed* in the Christian sense of the word."[4] John Wesley was aware of at least some of his own shortcomings and limitations, and he keenly appreciated the fact that he was a "clay jar" being used of God.

Neither John Wesley's personal struggles nor our own weaknesses, however, prevent God from loving and working through us. All of God's servants have, to some extent, failed in life, but neither the betrayal by Judas nor the denial by Peter tells the real story of Jesus' Farewell Supper. John 13 proclaims the victory of God over evil and human weakness, and the determination of God to work in us and through us.

If you are using this study in the season of Lent, you are also aware of the coming season of Easter. As you prepare for Easter, you may want to take stock of your strengths and weaknesses, and confess your shortcomings and failures. When rightly understood, failures and struggles help each of us stay humble and grateful for God's grace. As we love others humbly and without pretense, we reveal the glory of God and the truth of the gospel.

◼ Discussion Questions

1. The passages you have studied this week describe three different experiences of "failure": those of Judas, Peter, and Jesus. In what way did each fail? How did they, or did they not, overcome their failures?

2. In another sense, all of the disciples failed Jesus; they stood passively by as Judas went out into the night. Why did they miss the significance of what was happening? What does this say about the nature of evil and our response to it?

3. In 2 Corinthians 12:7-9, the Apostle Paul tells how he prayed for deliverance from a "thorn in the flesh"—that is, some kind of personal weakness or deficiency that he believed was harming his ministry. (Some scholars suggest that Paul may have been epileptic.) The Lord responded in a way that Paul had not expected, "My grace is sufficient for you, for power is made perfect in weakness." On that basis, Paul adopted a new attitude: "So, I will boast all the more gladly of my weaknesses, so that the power of Christ may dwell in me." Can you describe a time in your life when God worked through a failure or an impediment to bring about God's glory?

3
COMMISSIONED TO SERVE

My friend Tom starred as our high school fullback. As a junior, he rushed for close to 1000 yards and 60 points behind a veteran and talented senior line. The day the local paper named Tom "Player of the Year," the seniors were giving him some good-natured ribbing. "How are you going to do it again next year when we're gone, Tom?" they joked. "You think you'll get a thousand yards and ten touchdowns without us?"

Tom smiled and took the kidding in stride, but you could tell he was thinking, "How *will* I do as well next year?" Without a doubt, the juniors on our team who were getting ready to step up into those starting line positions lacked the size and talent of the seniors who were leaving. Only one of the starting linemen was returning, and Tom could only darkly imagine what it would mean to run behind an inexperienced and inferior line.

In spite of the circumstances, however, Tom did all right. In fact, he ran for over 1200 yards the next year and set a city record by scoring more than 180 points. Somehow those skinny, inexperienced linemen did the job (along with a lot of hard work and natural talent on Tom's part). A new coach came in and established an offensive scheme that maximized the talents of the new line and took advantage of Tom's strength and speed. He made us believe in what we could accomplish. Although less talented, this team scored more points and won more games than their more physically gifted predecessors.

The Departure of Jesus

Jesus' departure presents a much more difficult problem to the disciples than we faced losing our senior stars. Up to this point the disciples have depended heavily on Jesus, as well they should. They have seen his miracles, heard his teachings, and watched him pray; they have drawn courage, wisdom, and power from him. When Jesus says, "I am the way, and the truth, and the life" (Jn.14:6), he is claiming to reveal the essence of the Father in action and to offer God's salvation. Everything the disciples know about the power of the gospel centers in Jesus.

Now Jesus tells the disciples he is going away (Jn.14:3). The emphasis on the absolute unity between the Son and the Father (and all that this implies for the disciples) only makes the loss more acute. What is going to happen to the disciples without Jesus?

In this third week of our study, we can see how John 14 addresses these concerns. The chapter comforts, consoles, and exhorts the disciples. Far from being a time of despair, John 14 suggests that Jesus' departure will open a door of adventure and growth for the disciples. The disciples need not worry or be anxious. Their needs have been anticipated, and the future has been taken care of. They do not face loss, but great expectations.

Confidence for the Future

John 14 begins with Jesus' disconcerting announcement in 13:33, "Little children, I am with you only a little longer. You will look for me; and as I said to the Jews so now I say to you, 'Where I am going, you cannot come.' " Naturally, this statement shocked and disturbed the disciples. Many questions must have surfaced immediately. Where was Jesus going and why? Why would the disciples be unable to follow? What would happen to them if they were left behind?

Jesus' words are intended to comfort the disciples and to encourage them: "*Do not let your hearts be troubled. Believe in God, believe also in me*" (Jn. 14:1). In many ways this is an incredible statement. Belief in Jesus is laid equally alongside belief in God. His famous statement in John 14:6 only reinforces this idea, "I am the way, and the truth and the life. No one comes to the Father except through me." Faith in God has become defined as faith in Christ. Because the disciples have trusted and followed Jesus, they have believed and trusted God. The announcement of his departure may make the disciples wonder if they have made a mistake! They need not worry, however. They chose the only way to obey when they chose to trust Christ. Now they simply need to keep on believing.

In fact, Jesus tells the disciples that his departure has a specific purpose and destination. He is going to his "Father's house," where he will prepare a place for them (Jn.14:2). His Father has ample room for them. Jesus ultimately intends to return to the disciples to bring them to his Father's house and to be with them once again.

The confidence of the disciples is severely shaken by the idea that Jesus will leave them soon. Their lives have been so tied up in being *with* him, what will they do *without* him? In answer to these questions, Jesus points them back to the central claim of the gospel: The Son uniquely reveals the Father to those who believe in him. This fact does not change with the cross and the resurrection. The disciples' faith in and relationship with Jesus will continue to be the source of their life and salvation, even as Jesus departs. They are to go on trusting in him as the Son of God, whether he is present with them or waiting for them.

The disciples are being called back to their original faith in Christ. What Peter confessed in John 6:68-69 remains true: "Lord, to whom can we go? You have the words of eternal life. We have come to believe and know that you are the Holy One of God." Even as Jesus leaves the disciples in the crucifixion and the ascension, he remains their way to the Father and to life. His departure allows him to prepare their heavenly place and to come again to them.

Most of the time we hear this passage in the context of a funeral. Preachers typically apply this to the Christian hope of seeing our loved ones again and being reunited with them. Although this is not inappropriate, the main emphasis of the passage directs itself more toward the living than the dead. Jesus is trying to give the disciples hope and confidence for the future. Despite Jesus' death and departure, God's will is still being worked out through faith in him. The hope of the disciples is our hope. We do not live in a void, but in the context of a divine plan with a purpose and a destination. There is a house to which we are going that belongs to God, and Christ will take us there. In the meantime, our confidence rests in Christ, and our peace comes from our hope in him. We do not see Christ, but we still trust in him because he is still working for us and in us.

The Commission

Having given the disciples hope for their future, Jesus turns to the present. The idea that Jesus was about to leave them no doubt caused the disciples to feel confused and vulnerable. Not only would they miss Jesus himself, they would also miss all that he had done. Who would perform the miracles? Who would teach the multitudes? Who would proclaim the good news?

Jesus provides an outrageous answer to these questions: "*The one who believes in me will also do the works that I do and, in fact, will do greater works than these, because I am going to the Father*" (Jn. 14:12). These verses commission the disciples to carry on the ministry of Jesus. The disciples will "succeed" to the business, so to speak, and are expected not merely to do what Jesus did, but to do more.

We wonder, "In what sense could the disciples do 'greater works' than Jesus?" "Greater works" cannot mean more spectacular works. It would be hard to top the resurrection of Lazarus or the healing of the man born blind. It makes more sense to think that "greater" applies to the *scope* of the disciples' ministry.

Years ago I heard Dr. John Stott explain this passage, and his insights seem to me to hold true. While Jesus was alive, people had to go to him for everything. If Jesus were still alive, imagine the numbers of people trying to get to him for a word or a prayer! In his time, Jesus healed perhaps hundreds of people, and taught and preached to thousands. However, even these great numbers represent only a fraction of the people who were alive in his day; they represent an even smaller fraction of the present-day world population. The incarnation limited the geographical and personal influence of Jesus to the land of Judea and its people.

What happened after Easter bears witness to the "greater works" of the disciples. Within a generation, Christian churches had spread to the corners of the Roman empire and beyond. Jesus fed 5000 people at one meal. Within a generation, Christians fed the poor and helped the needy on an even larger scale. Jesus healed ten lepers at one time. Within a generation, Christians had developed a reputation for praying for the sick and caring for their needs all over the Roman world. Peter's first sermon at Pentecost had an impact in Jerusalem that was just as significant as the Sermon on the Mount in terms of the numbers of people reached. By the end of the book of Acts, the church at Antioch had become as influential as Jerusalem, and many more churches had begun to dot the Mediterranean world.

The church today carries on this commission. While our healing ministry may not have as much of the spectacular quality that marked Jesus' ministry, churches have founded thousands of hospitals and healing agencies all over the world. In many places, not only do Christian facilities and healthcare workers provide the best medical care; often Christian ministries provide the *only* care available. Millions of people meet weekly to hear the Word proclaimed and taught. Similar numbers of people have food and care because Christians reach out to the poor and hungry.

The faithful church does multiply the work of Jesus. As individuals, our contributions may seem slight, but in the aggregate we do fulfill Jesus' prediction of "greater works."

What about the death of Jesus and the redemptive nature of that sacrifice? Can we say in any sense that the church does a work greater than that? The church does *not* repeat the unique nature of the death of Christ—but we do proclaim it and share it. The crucified and risen Christ also appears alive in the lives and faith of Christians and, as a result, the power of the cross reaches and touches more and more people. We do not change the significance of the cross, but we do bear our own crosses. We are also given the privilege of participating in the sufferings of Christ so that the life of Christ might be proclaimed and shared through us. The witness of the Christian community as the body of Christ expands the reach of God's salvation from the small number of disciples at the foot of the cross to the whole world.

The Promise to Hear Our Prayers

From a historical perspective, we can see the church fulfilling, at least to some degree, the bold commission of Jesus. However, we could forgive the disciples if they found the thought of taking over the ministry of Jesus a bit intimidating! After all, Jesus could claim unity with the Father and identity with the works of God. They could claim no such thing. How could Jesus ever expect the disciples to do what he had done?

The success of others can intimidate us. While I worked at First United Methodist Church of Tulsa, visitors from other churches would often come by and quiz us about our programs and activities. As we explained and demonstrated the wide variety of ministries and people that made up our church, the visitors would often shrink back into their chairs and shake their heads.

You could tell they were thinking, "How could we ever do all that?" We constantly reminded them, "What you see here today is the result of more than twenty years of renewal and growth in this church. You are not going to start at the level it took us twenty years to reach. All you want to do is find the one or two ideas you can use right now and concentrate on those. We can give you some ideas of where you want to go and how to get there. It will take time, planning, and prayer to actually get going." We could help them develop a plan, but they had to make the plan work.

John 14 develops a plan for the disciples for carrying out the commission of Jesus. The first key to that plan lies in developing a relationship with God like Jesus' relationship to the Father. Jesus stresses in 14:10-12 that his works did not come out of his own intrinsic power, but out of the relationship he had with the Father. Note his words in 14:10f, "The words that I say to you I do not speak on my own; but the Father who dwells in me does his works. Believe that I am in the Father and the Father is in me." The power of Jesus to perform miracles and to minister flows from his relationship with the Father.

This suggests that the disciples must in some way form a similar relationship with God if they are to carry on the ministry of Jesus. In John 14:13-14, Jesus promises exactly such a relationship: "I will do whatever you ask in my name, so that the Father may be glorified in the Son. If in my name you ask me for anything, I will do it." Essentially, Jesus promises the disciples that he will hear their prayers and answer them. This is not an unconditional promise, but when the disciples find themselves in need and pray to God for help, Jesus will ensure that their prayers are heard and answered.

If the very God of creation hears your prayers and responds to them, what could offer more encouragement? What would we not attempt if we knew that God would be there to strengthen and empower us? Christians throughout the ages have witnessed answered prayers. This has not always made their lives easy, but God has answered prayers to make ministry possible, even in very difficult situations.

Lance Webb shares with us his own path of learning to pray:

> I have learned that when I ask for understanding, for wisdom, for insight in order that I may fulfill God's will—the real purpose of my life—I receive it.
>
> I have learned that when I seek and knock for courage, strength, and adequacy to be at my best in the fulfillment of my true mission, I always find the door opened with power to use my talents in a more remarkable way than I ever imagined.
>
> This is not only my testimony but the witness of countless ordinary persons as well as those whom the world calls extraordinary. The greatest achievements are not always to those with the most natural talents but to those whose prayers are the open doors to the full use of the small talent they possess.[5]

Does this mean that God will answer any prayer? The qualification Jesus makes here needs some explanation. Prayers given "in the name of Jesus" will be answered. This does not suggest some magical formula. Merely to end a prayer with the words, "In the name of Jesus we ask this" does not guarantee answers to prayer. The phrase "in the name of" had a legal and technical meaning in the first century. You could certify another person as your agent. Your agent could then use your name as your legal representative. To speak "in the name of" a person meant that you were acting under his or her orders in accordance with the commission given by the person to you. To pray "in the name of Jesus" means that we believe that we are seeking help to execute the commission given to us through the disciples to carry on the ministry of Jesus. What we are seeking in prayer would not be for ourselves, but for what we believe we need in order to do the works Jesus did. Our petitions would have to be consistent with the nature and call of Christ before we could pray "in the name of Jesus."

Jesus promises that the prayers of those who are carrying out his work will be heard. We have no promise that selfish petitions must be answered by God (except maybe by a "No!"). When we are not sure how to pray, we have to be open to a variety of answers from God. Jesus is promising, however, that we will have God's attention and God's power to carry out the commission he is giving us. We are invited to pray confidently for God's help in doing Christ's work.

The Promise of the Spirit

Alongside this assurance that Jesus will respond to the prayers of the disciples comes another promise—the promise of the Holy Spirit. As Jesus mediated the Father's presence for the disciples in the past (Jn. 14:9-10), the Holy Spirit will mediate the presence of Jesus and the Father for the disciples in the future (Jn.14:20, 23). Jesus tells the disciples, "I will not leave you orphaned" (Jn.14:18)—and the presence of the Spirit will be for them the ongoing experience of Christ.

Having walked for three years with Christ and enjoyed his constant presence and support, the disciples must have been frightened by the suggestion that they would now be on their own. Having depended on the wisdom, power, and courage of Jesus for so long, they now face a time of relying on their own resources.

We all depend on a network of relationships to support and encourage us. If you have ever been cut off from a key relationship, you know the sense of loss and the drain of energy that can cause. As a seventeen-year-old high school graduate, I went to Wyoming to work in the oil fields to earn money for college.

I arrived in Casper and found that I was six weeks too young to work on a rig. As a result, I was forced to live in a small motel on the edge of town, working in the equipment yard for minimum wages. I was without friends or family for the first time in my life. The loneliness seemed almost physical. As my natural self-confidence ebbed, I became depressed, so I quickly decided to return home. Out on my own for the first time, I felt small and vulnerable.

On a personal level, the presence and support of people make it possible for us to make it through life. On a spiritual level, the Holy Spirit acts to give us an inner sense or experience of the presence and support of God. We do not have to wait until after death to go to the Father's house; Jesus tells us that in the meantime he and the Father will make their "home" within us (Jn.14:23).

Anna Reynalds lived in Cornwall in the early days of the Methodist movement. In many ways she was an ordinary Christian who was known by only her close associates while she was alive and was quickly forgotten by succeeding generations. In her journal, she witnesses to a sense of God's presence:

> While praying the Lord to keep me while in the world I felt those words sweetly applied, "I will never leave thee nor forsake thee, abide in Me." Each day since I have had such a humbling sense of His loving presence as often crushes the animal frame beneath its [weight], from morning to night I feel as if [I am] at the feet of my blessed Lord. O help me to preserve this abiding witness of Thy presence.[6]

Anna Reynalds experienced a taste of the presence of God. She was allowed a glimpse of the glory of heaven for a time in her life. At other times, when life became difficult and when God did not seem as close, she never doubted the reality of God's love

for her and the promise of life with Christ. The Holy Spirit functions in this way to give us an assurance of God's presence and
reality in our lives. This sense of "God with us" encourages us
and supports us in our daily walk and faith.

John further tells us that the Holy Spirit helps us remember
and apply the teachings of Jesus in our lives: "[T]he Holy Spirit,
whom the Father will send in my name will teach you everything, and remind you of all that I have said to you" (Jn. 14:26).
Scripture has an unusual ability to strengthen, guide, and direct
the Christian. John understands the words of Jesus to be the
words of God. For those seeking to carry on the ministry of
Jesus, no greater guide exists than Jesus' teachings in scripture.

The Holy Spirit works uniquely in scripture to clarify our
ideas and to define what is happening to us and what we should
do in response. Once I walked into a hospital room and found a
parishioner, Virginia, resting with an open Bible on her bed.
Fighting a long battle with cancer, she had been suddenly hospitalized again. In the hasty trip she was able to bring only a few
personal items, but she did bring her Bible. She eagerly showed
me where she had been reading, telling me, "God gave me what I
needed." Together we read the words of the Psalmist:

*The Lord is your keeper; the Lord is your shade at your
right hand. The sun shall not strike you by day, nor the
moon by night. The Lord will keep you from all evil; he will
keep your life. The Lord will keep your going out and your
coming in from this time on and forevermore (Ps. 121:5-8).*

Her sudden return to the hospital and the ongoing pain and
misery of the cancer treatment had almost beaten Virginia, but
the words of the psalm drew her back to faith and confidence,
and to a sense of God's caring presence for her.

In times of stress and difficulty, the Holy Spirit works to help
us remember scripture that we have stored in our memory, and to

take strength and guidance from it. As we read scripture, some-times a verse will jump off the page and grab us and demand a decision. Ken Kinghorn, Professor of Church History at Asbury Theological Seminary, tells about a professor who had begun to get a bit lazy in his faith. One day, as he was reading his Bible, a verse from Galatians leapt out at him, "Do not be deceived; God is not mocked, for you reap whatever you sow" (Gal. 6:7). Immediately the professor felt a sense of conviction. He was sowing very little; therefore he should not be surprised that little was happening in his life. Dr. Kinghorn continues the man's story:

> As God's Spirit helped me to face myself, I surrendered my lethargy to Christ and asked him to forgive me. I prayed that God would fill me with a new energy and anoint me with a new vision. He answered my prayer. With his help I began to tackle projects I had been putting off. I found myself actually enjoying the work I had been avoiding.[7]

Through scripture, the Holy Spirit alternately comforts us or exhorts us, depending on our need. We find real and practical help and guidance for living out the Christian life as we prayer-fully seek God's guidance in the Word.

Obedience

Also interwoven in John 14 are instructions on obedience which are repeated in various forms:

> If you love me, you will keep my commandments
> (Jn. 14:15).
> They who have my commandments and keep them
> are those who love me (Jn. 14:21).

Those who love me will keep my word. . . Whoever does not love me does not keep my words (Jn.14:23-24).

These calls to love and obedience tie together the promise of the Holy Spirit and God's promise to hear prayers "in the name of Jesus." Implicitly, the commission and call to the ministry of Jesus, as well as the tools given for that ministry, come to those who want to love and obey Christ.

The emphasis on the commandments of Christ seems unusual, given the singular lack of any list of commands. In fact, in John we can find only two commandments. John 14:1 gives the first commandment: Believe in me. John 13:34 gives the other: Love one another as I have loved you.

Fulfilling the commission that Jesus gives the disciples in John 14 really boils down to obeying these two commandments. We must believe in Christ and boldly proclaim this faith. The promise of eternal life, the experience of the Holy Spirit, the forgiveness of sins, and all the other promises depend on faith in Christ. Jesus called people to faith in himself so that people could really experience the life of God. Through the disciples, others came to faith. Through a chain of faithful witnesses, we, too, receive and enjoy the good news of Christ. Now we proclaim our faith to others so they can experience the life Christ gives. Serving Christ means believing in Christ and sharing this faith with others.

Our message about Christ is tied to our actions and to our words. Our witness to Christ and our witness of love validate and complement one another. As a young teacher, my wife had students come to her and say, "There is something different about you. Tell me what it is." Whether evidenced in Mother Teresa or a compassionate teacher motivated by Christ, the desire to love and serve others witnesses to people. Through us, others get a glimpse of the glory of heaven, even as the disciples witnessed this in Christ. Jesus has commissioned the disciples, and through them has commissioned us, to carry on his ministry of proclamation and love in our own world.

Therefore, those commissioned to carry on the work of Christ accept these commands and seek to live them out. John 14 promises us that we do not live and work in our own strength. We live, believe, and work in the presence and glory of the Father, Son, and Holy Spirit. Our prayers "in the name of Jesus" are heard and answered. The Holy Spirit lives in us and through us so that we experience the peace and presence of Jesus, as well as remember and apply his teachings, and show his glory to others. This is Jesus' promise.

Jesus is telling us that the church is amply equipped to carry on his work, and to do even greater work. Although church history is filled with the mistakes and shortcomings of individual Christians and institutions, over and over again, new people have come into faith and life. Millions have been fed, healed, and renewed through the work of ordinary Christians. Perhaps the greatest witness to the truth of this chapter lies in the ongoing effectiveness of the ministry of the church.

If God has used flawed people of the past to fulfill this commission, then why would God not use us? The same tools for ministry that were available to the disciples and to the saints of the ages still exist for us: prayer, the Holy Spirit, and obedience. Especially during the season of Lent, we can recommit ourselves with renewed dedication to take up the work of Christ as well as the tools that Jesus has given us to carry on his ministry. This is what Jesus told us to believe and to do. It is up to us to pray, to seek the presence and guidance of the Holy Spirit, and to obey as we carry out the work of Jesus in our own world.

◼ *Discussion Questions*

1. Have you ever experienced having to face a difficult situation without the presence of a friend or loved one to support you? If you can, describe that experience in writing and share it with the others in your group.

2. To encourage the disciples in the face of his impending departure, Jesus emphasized that he is one with the Father and the Spirit. He wanted them to know that God would continue to be the very One they had come to know and trust in him (Jesus). What discouraging ideas or notions about God do you suppose Jesus wanted to rule out by making this profession so emphatic?

3. In view of the discussion on pages 37-39, give some examples of prayer "in Jesus' name." Does praying in this way mean that we never ask for anything that we want or need in our own lives?

4. The promise of Jesus that his disciples would do "even greater works" than he had done probably sounds a bit audacious to some of us. Do you think Christians today are bold enough about testing the reliability of this promise in their own experience? Why or why not? What could you do to test the promise more fully in your experience?

4
HARD TIMES DISCIPLESHIP

I woke up with a start when the phone rang, feeling as if it must be the middle of the night. Actually, the clock read just past midnight as I picked up the phone. On the other end of the line, my friend was asking me to come over to his house. His wife—we'll call her Mary—had just died.

The news did not surprise me. Seven years earlier, she had been hospitalized just before the birth of their first child. Tests had located a brain tumor. Days after the birth of their daughter, she underwent her first operation. The news from the surgery came back as bad as possible: it was cancer, the doctors could not get all of it, and it would come back.

Over the next seven years, this brave woman underwent more operations, chemotherapy, and a slow, steady decline. Mary was a bright and independent woman, and her illness tested her faith and temperament. She had to give up the job she loved. She reached a point where she had to turn over the cooking and the care of the house to others—and even the care of her only child. Mary was a fighter by nature, but this was not a fair fight. The disease had all the advantages, and Mary was never given a real chance to win.

The grind of the fight ate away at her spirit. At one point, I was visiting her in the rehabilitation ward of the hospital after another surgery. She was worn out and frustrated. Thin and losing control over her own body, Mary wanted to know what the purpose of all this suffering could be.

I told her as truthfully as I could what I thought. Sometimes we suffer because of the mistakes we make or others make.

Sometimes suffering and hard times give us the opportunity to grow and develop character. In Mary's case, any character development should have been accomplished long ago. Neither of these two "easy" answers for suffering seemed to fit here, so I told her that sometimes suffering just *is*. We live in a fallen and imperfect world. We cannot always find a purpose for suffering. In these cases, we have a choice—either to go through suffering with God or by our ourselves. As hard as it is, it is still much better to suffer with God.

"Well," said Mary, "I made the decision to stay with God a long time ago. It's just hard to keep on going."

All the way through her long ordeal, Mary did witness to her faith in God. She stayed as active in church activities as her strength, helping and praying for others as she could. She also became a focal point of service for others. Friends brought over meals throughout the illness. They prayed for her and with her. Many were touched by her life and by her death. She had a tough faith, and everyone who knew Mary loved her for her strength and perseverance.

The tone of Jesus' words to the disciples turns darker in John 15. The darker tone suggests that the church of the fourth Gospel was beginning to face times of difficulty and persecution. The church would need to know how to make it through these dark times. We will study this theme often in the second half of our study as the need for perseverance dominates the next chapters. In John 16:1-4*b*, the disciples are warned that they face excommunication from the synagogues and even death for their faith. Such suffering always poses a challenge for faith. If God is good and powerful, surely God will take care of those people who seek to love and to follow the divine will. Yet from Job and the Psalmist to the disciples, the righteous have at times suffered in their righteousness. Often, as they suffer, they see no clear relief in sight. Where is God when the righteous suffer? What are the righteous to do? To answer these questions, John reaches

back into the teachings of Jesus and reflects on the words of
Jesus in a new light.

The Vinedresser, the Vine, and the Branches

Scholars have called John 15:1-8 the only parable in the
Gospel of John. The portrait of the vinedresser and his vine
really functions as more of an extended allegory rather than as
a true parable. The meaning of the picture Jesus is drawing in
these verses lies in the relationships between the vinedresser and
the vine, and between the vine and the branches. Jesus must
draw out the significance of these relationships and apply them
to the situation of the disciples, in order to give them guidance
through their own tough times.

Jesus tells us here that his Father functions as a vinedresser,
while Jesus himself operates in the role of the vine, and the disciples are the branches in the vine. As the vinedresser, the Father
superintends and cares for the vineyard. Like any good farmer,
he has a goal for his vineyard—to bear as much fruit as possible.
Like any good vinedresser, he must prune his vines, cutting off
branches that will not bear fruit and further pruning any branches
that do bear fruit.

As members of an agrarian society, the disciples understand
the need for this. A branch that does not bear fruit takes energy
and sustenance from the vine that could otherwise be dedicated
to growing grapes. Even fruit-bearing branches need pruning.
Excess leaves and smaller branches take food and energy away
from the grape-growing process. The goal of any good vineyard
owner is to make each vine use as much of its growth as possible
in making grapes, and as little as possible in extraneous leaves
and branches.

Jesus quickly draws the significance of this for the disciples.
First, he points out that what happens to the vine comes through
the plan of the vineyard keeper. The pruning of branches does

not reflect a haphazard decision, but the careful concern of the vinedresser for the fruit of the vine. Just as the vinedresser directs the care of the vine, so the Father is still directing history, even when times are hard.

In one sense, Jesus' example of vine and branches suggests a sobering fact. Branches on a vine have only two possible fates. Either they do not bear fruit, are cut off from the vine, and are tossed into the fire, or they do bear fruit, are pruned, and "cleansed" (Jn.15:3). All branches experience times of being cut back—it is only the nature of the cutting process that varies.

The implication for discipleship could not be clearer: All Christians can expect times of difficulty. Christians do not have to wonder whether struggles will come (they will), but only what to do with the hard times they will inevitably face. No option is given for an easy way out. Growth implies pruning, but no growth is worse.

In this sense, the question we tend to ask in the midst of suffering starts in the wrong place. We want to ask, "Why me?" We assume too quickly in the midst of difficulties that something must be wrong with us or with God. Yet in the midst of our troubles, suggestions that we deserve our suffering—or that God has a plan for our hard times—seem hollow and unsatisfying. We feel as if God, or someone, is picking on us. In truth, the real question Christ wants us to ask in the midst of trouble is not "Why me?" but "What should I do?" The "why" of our hard times often remains a mystery. The challenge for us is to remain faithful.

The passage further implies that disciples tend to fall into two types—those that do "bear fruit" and those that do not. Jesus never defines what he means by "fruit." Some have suggested that "fruit" means leading others into a life of faith. Others have pointed toward the development of Christian character and values. The lack of definition suggests that the specifics were not the point. The New Testament does not understand or accept the idea of discipleship without results. In some sense, being a Christian must make a difference in our lives and point to the goodness and greatness of the God we say we follow.

The key to bearing fruit, we are told, lies in abiding or remaining (Jn. 15:4, 7). The vine supplies the water and the nourishment that enable the branch to bear fruit. Only as the branch remains connected to the vine is fruit-bearing possible. Detach the branch from the vine, and the branch will wither. Keep the branch connected to the vine, and the branch will bear fruit.

Christ is the vine. Disciples who remain connected with Christ will bear fruit. Disciples who do not remain in Christ can do nothing (Jn.15:5). Again, Jesus does not define specifically what it means to "abide" or remain in him. The point must be to maintain an ongoing relationship with Christ. We have many tools available to keep our relationship with Christ vital and growing: worship, Christian fellowship, the study of scripture, Christian service, and prayer spring to mind. The fruitful Christian uses some or all of these to keep a vital relationship going.

We sense in this verse the real danger to the disciples— not that Christians will fail to bear fruit, but that they will allow themselves to be cut off from Christ. All those who abide in Christ *do* bear fruit. Those who are unfruitful owe their barren-ness to cutting themselves off from Christ: "I am the vine and you are the branches. Those who abide in me and I in them bear much fruit, because apart from me you can do nothing" (Jn. 15:5).

Why does John 15 raise the possibility of being cut off from the vine? Christ tells the disciples in John 16:1, "I have said these things to you to keep you from stumbling." Hard times and opposition make some people give up. When hard times hit, some people cut themselves off from their community of faith.

Reflect for a moment about why this happens. We all want to look our best at church. We have a natural desire to appear to be strong, independent persons. When something difficult comes up in life, we pull into ourselves, trying to solve our own

problems. However, this attempt at self-salvation too often leads
to unforeseen and far-reaching consequences.

During the recent recession in the oil industry, we saw a
recurring pattern among people who lost their jobs. Out of
wounded pride, they would stop going to church in order to avoid
embarrassing questions. In doing so, they cut themselves off
from people who would support and care for them. They then
became more easily depressed and defeated by the difficulties of
unemployment and the job search. The final result was often to
become more withdrawn and less involved, putting more distance
between themselves and their friends—and their faith. Without
the support of faith and church, other problems began to domi-
nate their lives.

Many churches started "Job Ministries" to help combat this
syndrome. When individuals lost their jobs, people in the ministry would invite them to a support group. In the group, they
would meet others like themselves and be able to share their
struggles with one another. They also helped each other write
new résumés, develop job leads, and prepare for interviews.
Most important, they helped each other deal with the disappointment of not getting a job, yet keep on trying. The encouragement
of the group also kept the people in worship and in relationship
to Christ. Far from causing embarrassment to them, their faith
became an ongoing support to men and women suffering from
the dislocation of the oil industry.

The results of the Job Ministry were dramatic. Those persons who remained in relationship to the church and to Christ
handled their disappointments and struggles better than those
who did not participate. Moreover, they found positive things to
do even while struggling with the loss of their jobs. People in
the Jobs Ministry not only helped each other find jobs, they
made themselves available around the church to help in many
ways—with the sick and homebound, with small jobs needed by
the elderly, and in many other areas. Although hurting, they

found ways to keep going—through their faith, and through their relationship with Christ and with one another that gave them meaning and significance.

Those who withdrew tended to struggle more. This was not true for all of them, but they frequently brooded more on their own problems and were less involved with the needs of others. Missed job opportunities hit them harder, and they struggled more to keep on going and to try to find work.

When hard times and struggles hit, most of us are tempted to lose faith, to withdraw, and to cut ourselves off. John 15 warns us that such a course can be disastrous. Branches that try to live apart from the vine wither and die and are thrown into the fire. The key to long-term health for a branch lies in remaining firmly connected to the vine. In the midst of hard times, disciples need to work hard to maintain their relationship with Christ. Christ and the community of faith can keep us healthy as long as we maintain our relationship.

Ironically, in the long run, hard times can even *help* Christians. Difficult times make us concentrate on priorities and cut back on anything that takes our energy away from what is vital in life. God can use the suffering in our lives to "prune" us and to make us healthier for the long run.

The loss of jobs made many of our members go through a time of reassessment and change. The good life had led most to fill their days with activities and to buy the fun, material things available to North Americans. Now, faced with less money, they began to concentrate on different things. Relationships with friends and families became more important. Some learned in a new way that who they were as persons did not depend on what they owned, but on the quality of their lives. They became more empathetic and actively involved in the needs of others. Their struggle led them to become more committed to Christ and more involved in their faith—and more generous to others even as they had less to give.

Hard times and difficulties pose a challenge for the Christian. In your need, where will you turn? If you turn in to yourself, you may separate yourself from Christ and from his resources. The failure to remain in Christ can lead you to wither and die. If you turn to Christ and faith in the midst of struggle, you may find that the hardest times become opportunities for growth. You may have to reevaluate your priorities and let go of some things that you formerly valued. However, you may in turn find your faith growing and your usefulness to Christ growing, just as your own resources seem to dwindle.

Reinterpreting the Promises of Christ

Like Jesus' first disciples, when life is throwing bricks our way, we may suddenly call into question everything that heretofore we trusted. After losing a job, a confident person may feel insecure. In the midst of chronic pain, the naturally outgoing person may become quiet and withdrawn. When life gets hard, our emotional, physical, and spiritual resources all too quickly become depleted. We feel defeated . . . deserted . . . depressed.

In John 14, when Jesus called the disciples to carry on his work, he also offered them resources and promised to help them. Now, John 15 promises resources for disciples in the midst of increasingly hard times. Indeed, John 15 in many ways parallels John 14. The same or similar promises are adapted to the new, more stressful context. In the midst of times of struggle, the words of Jesus find new meaning.

For those who feel defeated, John 15:7 repeats the promise that God will hear the prayers of the disciples, but now puts the promise in conditional form, "If you abide in me, and my words abide in you, ask for whatever you wish, and it will be done for you." The chief danger of hard times is giving up, but God hears the prayers of those who abide.

Jesus' promise in John 14:13-14 to hear prayers makes no mention of abiding. Instead, the emphasis there is on the commission to continue his work, to obey. Obedience in hard times, however, means hanging on in spite of resistance or trouble. In the midst of struggles and disappointment, we can easily get discouraged and give up. Typically, when things are going badly, we pray, "Lord get us out of this mess!" When we are not immediately delivered from our problems, we may become angry or lose confidence. We are tempted to stop praying and give up. Nevertheless, John 15:7 promises that those who continue to abide and pray will find that God answers their prayer. The timing of the answer is left open, but we are assured God will respond.

People going through hard times also find that the ongoing grind eats up their emotional resources. People who face long-term unemployment or illness may begin to feel depressed. When things are not going well, we naturally question ourselves. Have we done something wrong? Is God mad at us? Jesus assures the disciples, "As the Father has loved me, so I have loved you; abide in my love. If you keep my commandments, you will abide in my love, just as I have kept my Father's commandments and abide in his love" (Jn. 15:9-10).

These verses read very much like the promise in 14:21, but in John 14 the disciples are told that those who obey Christ's commands prove that they love Jesus, so the Father *will love* them. However, John 15 begins with the fact that the Father *has loved* them. To continue in that love, the disciples need only to continue to obey. John 14 looks forward to the disciples' obedience. John 15 consoles them in the midst of the battle.

John 15 does make one significant change from John 14. In both instances, Jesus links the promise with his desire to forewarn the disciples. But in John 14:27, faithful disciples are promised to share Jesus' *peace*, while in John 15:11 the distressed disciples are told they will share his *joy*. The difference again reflects the change of context. For those called to carry on the work of Jesus, the promise of peace suggests that the disciples can expect a sense of security and fulfillment as they carry out their commission. Jesus' "peace" came from his sure knowledge of his own mission and from his relationship with the Father. The disciples could share a similar confidence.

In the context of opposition and conflict, on the other hand, Jesus shifted the emphasis to "joy." This does not imply that the disciples enjoyed conflict! Jesus' joy came in his ultimate vindication as God's Son. The resurrection and ascension turned the sorrow of the cross into joy. In the same way, the disciples could look at the resurrection and see the promise of their own vindication. In the midst of conflict and hard times, "peace" may seem like a foreign concept, but the resurrection of Jesus could inspire and motivate the disciples. They, too, could expect that God would take them through the hard times to victory and joy.

Here, as with the other promises, the key lies in not giving up. Joy comes to those who "abide." None of this suggests that discipleship involves missing the hard times. Because hard times are sure to come, the promises are reinterpreted in anticipation of a more difficult future. The promises still hold. God will still hear the prayers of the faithful. God will still love those who obey the commandments. God will still be with those who trust Jesus. But in the midst of the struggle, the promises of God apply only to those who do not give up, who are not defeated by the struggle or cowed by opposition.

Reinterpreting the Example of Christ

As John 15 takes and reapplies the promises of Christ to the context of conflict and opposition, it also takes the example of Christ and makes new sense of it. In John 15:12, the disciples are told again, "Love one another as I have loved you." This virtually repeats his command given in John 13:34, but now

Jesus adds definition to the nature of that love. "No one has greater love than this, to lay down one's life for one's friends" (Jn. 15:13). More clearly than ever, we see that Jesus' sacrifice on the cross has become the measure of true love.

Why does Jesus refer to the cross more explicitly in John 15? It may be that more Christians were being called to pay this ultimate price as John was writing the fifteenth chapter. John 14 expects Christians to give sacrificially of themselves. John 15 knows that Christians are dying for each other. In the midst of this type of personal sacrifice, the church needs to hear that their deaths have meaning.

No one expects or wants the disciples to seek out martyrdom, but to care enough for others to put yourself at physical risk is truly to love as Jesus loved. Such people Jesus calls not only his servants but his friends. In a sense, they have become his peers in serving love.

Years ago I attended a missionary conference where Dr. Glenn Estruth spoke. Dr. Estruth served at a Methodist hospital in Zaire, a continuously troubled country. He told of being harassed and menaced by soldiers and bandits as he went about caring for people in the name of Christ. He went through hardships and dangers that amazed pale suburbanites such as myself, yet he willingly went back to Zaire after his furlough because he was needed there to care for people and to witness to Christ.

The next year we heard the shocking news that Dr. Estruth had been taken by soldiers and killed. Love for God and love for people led him back to a dangerous and troubled land. He did not want to die, but he took the risk of death to serve others. Truly, this was love as Jesus loved.

We may struggle to understand why people would kill a helper and healer like Dr. Estruth. However, we should not be surprised. In John 15:20, Jesus warns his disciples, "Remember the word that I said to you, 'Servants are not greater than their masters.' If they persecuted me, they will persecute you." Here

the words of 13:16 are repeated and given a very different meaning. In John 13, the disciples are urged to emulate Jesus' service
because they are servants and he is master. Here they are warned
that they will be treated like the master they emulate. If people
hated and persecuted Christ, they will also hate and persecute
those who love like Christ. Faith can be very threatening to those
who have none.

I had the privilege of meeting Vasile Talos, leader of the
Romanian Baptist Church. During the communist regime, his
small church was harassed and threatened in many ways. He
himself was routinely picked up and questioned, and even beaten
on occasion. Why? Were the Baptists plotting against the state?
Did they have power or wealth to threaten the communist party?

Authoritarian regimes dislike any kind of opposition or inde-
pendence. People who have allegiances beyond the state threaten
the power of the government. Moreover, the ultimate tools of
the totalitarian state are fear and death. Those who do not fear
death, and indeed are willing to die for their faith, threaten such a
state. Every dictatorship—whether of the right or the left—fears
people of faith because faith like this takes away the state's ability to control people.

As North Americans, such tales of persecution may not seem
pertinent to our comfortable lives. However, even here, on a
personal level we may also experience opposition and conflict
because of our faith. Individuals, like governments, distrust
those who seem "different." People with enthusiasm, love, and
commitment will naturally threaten some people.

As Jesus was hated by some in his day for being different
and for threatening the status quo, so Christians today who are
serious in their faith will from time to time find opposition
and resistance. Even good deeds can draw opposition, but
this should not surprise us, since this also happened to Christ.

A friend of mine took up a college ministry that by all
accounts had been moribund. He created new programs, Bible

studies, community outreach opportunities, and mission trips. The college ministry began to supply youth pastors for summer programs in small churches. The number of students involved mushroomed.

However, this did not make everyone happy. Some criticized the outreach methods. Others attacked my friend's motivation. He was committed to certain ideas, and those who disagreed with his ideas attacked him. Jesus' example warns us that this will happen. If they attacked Jesus for healing the sick and visiting the outcast, we can be sure that even our own attempts to minister will bring opposition at times.

Understandably, many good people simply wear out in the midst of trouble and opposition. What amazes us are those who do not. Some of those who suffer the most seem to have the strongest witness to the end. To a certain extent that only makes sense. Once you give up, the heat is off. Only those who never give up experience the full force of suffering. The fact that some people continue to keep the faith in the midst of the hardest imaginable circumstances creates awe in us.

We who are not suffering so obviously may be in the greatest danger. When I met the Reverend Talos, I expressed my admiration for his courage. He humbly and graciously waved off my words of praise. "I think," he said, "that you Americans may face difficulties much greater than I." Seeing my incredulity, he went on to explain, "You see, the lines were very clearcut for us. If we gave up, we lost all our faith. Without our faith we would be as hopeless and trapped as everyone else. But you are so comfortable. What does Christ have to offer you? I think the comfort of America is far more difficult than the persecution in Romania."

Reverend Talos' observations struck me as profoundly true. Comfort creates its own difficulty for the Christian. Most of our lives roll along so smoothly and easily that we are unprepared for stressful times. When difficulties come, we are untrained in real discipline and find giving up all the easier. We take our suffering more personally, as if God were out to get us, instead of seeing hard times as a normal part of the Christian life. We may become more vulnerable to the temptation to fall away under suffering, because suffering surprises us more.

During special seasons such as Lent, we sometimes make a sacrifice of personal denial. Through fasting or giving up some personal pleasure, we remind ourselves of the sacrifice of Christ. For Western Christians, the act of denying ourselves may have another purpose: to remind ourselves of the cost of following Christ and to prepare ourselves to abide and remain as we sometimes suffer for the privilege of faith. Lent can be a time when we ready ourselves for the difficult times of life and prepare ourselves not to give up easily when life becomes hard.

Comfortable Americans, saints, and martyrs—all must employ the same tools in living out the Christian life: obedience, prayer, love as Christ loved, and trust in the Holy Spirit. But most of all, the key to surviving both hard times and the seduction of comfortable times reverberates throughout this chapter. Never give up. Keep on being faithful. Abide in Christ.

◪ *Discussion Questions*

1. What sorts of difficulties or opposition do you, or others you know, face in life?

2. What tools do you use to "abide" in your Christian life? What helps you most in times of trouble?

3. Note the emphasis Jesus gives to his own example in this chapter. Do you think Jesus intends for us to be like him in every way? Explain.

4. Have you ever practiced a discipline of denial during Lent or at other times? Is there something you could do that would help you develop your determination to abide and to remain in Christ? Write down a sacrifice or discipline you intend to practice for Christ in the coming week, and sign your name under this as an indication of your commitment.

5
Overcoming in the Spirit

In Oklahoma we have a saying, "If you don't like the weather, just wait a minute and it will change." Indeed, the winds can come down from the north or up from the Gulf of Mexico and radically alter the day in just a few minutes. The black and menacing clouds of a thunderstorm can roll across a bright blue sky and make the day as dark as night. The wind will almost knock you down, and the rain will come down in torrents. Then it will all blow away and be bright and blue again, as if the storm had never happened.

Life changes as much as the weather in Oklahoma—and almost as fast. While the tempo of change in our time may be greater, change has always been with us. The England of John Wesley's day had many churches, but most had been built in rural settings, connected with the great manor houses. As the population shifted to the developing industrial towns, the church did not follow suit. The workers in the factories and mines lived differently and in different places from their farmer ancestors, and they were being neglected by the churches of their times.

George Whitefield hit upon a novel idea: Preach to people where they are. This meant preaching in the fields around the mines and factories as the workers walked to work in the early morning or in the late afternoon. The response amazed Whitefield—the workers responded to the good news hungrily. He called upon his teacher, friend, and mentor, John Wesley, to come and help, but, initially, Wesley hesitated. Preaching outside of the church seemed vulgar to him, and he confessed in his journal, "I should have thought the saving of souls almost a sin if it had not been done in a church" (March 31, 1739). But the next day, as Wesley was preaching on the Sermon on the Mount, it struck him that this was an example of field preaching! The following day, he took to the fields and began, reluctantly at first, but with growing enthusiasm, to preach where people were.[8]

The success of the Wesleyan movement in England reflected in some measure the ability of John Wesley and his co-workers to change. Typically, as they faced new situations and needs in their changing world, they responded by taking established ideas and forms and adapting them to new circumstances. At the same time, their innovations brought opposition and sometimes violence. Methodism has become so respectable that we strain to remember the hostility that Wesley and his methods faced in the beginning, but such negative reactions inevitably come with change. Change threatens us. Even change that helps people will meet with resistance from some.

As we begin this fifth week of our study, we need to reflect on the fact that any recommitment of our lives implies change, and change always raises problems. John 16 reflects the realization that Christians in those days were facing changing times. In part, as we saw in the last chapter, the times were becoming harsher and more dangerous. In another sense, however, the times were simply becoming different. In dealing with these changes, the Christians were concerned with meeting the new challenges, while being faithful to the truth of the gospel. In John 16, Jesus lifts up the work and guidance of the Holy Spirit to assure the disciples that they can meet the challenge of dangerous and changing times.

The Holy Spirit and Conflict

All the Gospels reflect a sequence of conflicts between Jesus and the ruling religious hierarchy. The priests and scribes viewed Jesus with doubt and concern because he seemed to compromise on two very basic issues. Jesus criticized contemporary views of the sabbath (Mk. 2:23-3:6; Jn. 5:16*a*), and few things were more fiercely protected in first-century Judaism than the sabbath. Jeremiah 17 had lifted up Israel's desecration of the sabbath as a key reason for their defeat at the hands of the Babylonians and the ensuing exile. When the nation was established again under Ezra and Nehemiah, the keeping of the sabbath became a prime concern (Neh. 13:15-22). Yet Jesus severely criticized the scribal approach to keeping the sabbath in his day, and this began the negative reaction to his teaching and ministry (Mk. 2:23-3:6; Jn. 5:16). When Jesus attacked the moneychangers in the temple (Jn. 2), this was interpreted as a threat to the temple itself and, by extension, to the priesthood and all those who depended on the temple for their livelihood. Most of all, the priests and scribes felt that some of Jesus' statements amounted to claiming equality with God (Jn. 5:18), and this claim threatened the peace (Jn. 11:50) and deserved death (Jn. 19:7).

The same opposition Jesus faced was now bearing down on his followers who proclaimed him as Lord. In the face of this opposition, Jesus spoke words of comfort to his disciples. In a nutshell, his message was this: As they stood up for him, the Holy Spirit would stand with them and help them!

> When the Advocate comes, whom I will send to you from the Father, the Spirit of truth who comes from the Father, he will testify on my behalf. You also are to testify because you have been with me from the beginning (Jn. 15:26-27).

> Nevertheless I tell you the truth: it is to your advantage that I go away, for if I do not go away, the Advocate will not come to you; but if I go, I will send him to you. And when he comes, he will prove the world wrong about sin and righteousness and judgment: about sin, because they do not believe in me; about righteousness, because

*I am going to the Father and you will see me no longer;
about judgment, because the ruler of this world has been
condemned (Jn. 16:7-11).*

The Greek word *Paraclete*, which the NRSV translates
"Advocate," is made up of two Greek words which mean "alongside of" and "called." This word is sometimes used to refer to a
defense counsel in a trial. In these verses the Spirit acts as an
advocate alongside the believer, complementing the work of the
faithful. In "trial" situations the believer does not stand alone.
The Holy Spirit will be there arguing with and for the faithful.

The second set of verses in 16:7-11 takes this a step further.
These verses visualize the trial as a contest between the world
and the faithful. In this trial the Holy Spirit does more than just
defend the faithful. The Advocate turns the table on the adver-
saries of God who are trying to destroy the witness of Christ.
Notice how the NRSV translates the action of the Holy Spirit:
"He will prove the world wrong about sin and righteousness and
judgment" (Jn.16:8). Other versions translate this verse a bit
differently, using the words *convict* or *convince* to describe the
action of the Spirit. The idea is this: As the world tries to convict
Christians for their faith in Christ, the Holy Spirit will actually
convict the world of sin and faithlessness. The Spirit does more
than act as defense attorney for the believer; the Advocate
prosecutes the world through the witness of the faithful.

These words offer encouragement to the disciples. They can
be confident that when they are attacked and even put on trial for
their faith, the Holy Spirit can reverse the situation. They will
never be simply helpless prisoners. Even in the midst of opposition and captivity, God can use the situation to convict and to
bring to faith the very people who are standing against them.

In this description of the work of the Holy Spirit, we can also
see an implied description of the work of the church. The world
needs to see proof of the resurrection in the life of the church.

The faith of the disciples will convince some people of the error of rejecting Jesus. The faithfulness of the disciples will point to the righteousness of Christ. The ability of the church to stand in the face of opposition without wavering will point to the final victory of Jesus and the judgment of Satan. In short, through the witness of the disciples, the enemies of faith will see the living Christ and some will be convicted themselves. Eventually, the world will understand the hopelessness of opposition to God and will choose faith.

Occasionally, we can document an experience where the Holy Spirit turns the tables on the accusers of the faithful. John Wesley records an occasion when the house where he was studying was surrounded by a mob. He brought in first one and then two more of his opponents, and spoke with them. These personal encounters left the ringleaders of the mob feeling differently about Wesley. Going out to the mob, Wesley agreed to go to a Justice of the Peace to see if he had done anything wrong. Along the way, a second, more unruly group joined the protesters, increasing the tension of the affair. Several people struck at Wesley. At this point, his original attackers turned and began to defend the man they had threatened. Wesley tells us:

> In the meantime my strength and my voice returned and I broke out aloud into prayer. And now the man who just before headed the mob turned and said, "Sir, I will spend my life for you; follow me and not one soul here will touch a hair of your head." Two or three of his fellows confirmed his words and got close to me immediately.[9]

Wesley returned home safely and credited the change of heart of the leaders of the mob to the work of God.

While most of us do not face mobs and violence (though some Christians do), we do, from time to time, face opposition. At times when we are sincerely seeking to serve God, we will run into people or situations that try us. People will doubt our motives or try to stop our ministry. In one local church, a woman felt the call of God to start a group to help teenage mothers. The group met in the church and learned basic mothering skills and health-care for infants, then sought to train and encourage these young women. The woman was surprised when members of the church approached her and asked her to move the group out of the church. These young women were not quite the kind of women the church members were used to having around. Their babies were noisy and created a mess. The members would feel more comfortable if they found another place to meet.

These verses encourage us not to lose heart in the face of such opposition. We are reminded that even opponents may be potential converts. The Holy Spirit can use our witness to our "enemies" (or to those who oppose us) to change their minds and to convict them of their attitudes. In conflict we are not left alone or without resources. We do not have to attack those who oppose us. The Holy Spirit can use our faith and our love to witness to them and to help them find Christ.

The Holy Spirit and Change

When times change, or situations change, people and institutions must change or die. In the 1950s, the March of Dimes was created to combat the threat of polio. With the development of the Salk and Sabin vaccines, the movement had to change its direction in order to continue to justify its existence. The move to concentrate on correcting and alleviating birth defects allowed the March of Dimes to maintain the most significant part of its original purpose (namely the medical problems of children), while adapting to success in dealing with the particular disease of polio.

The early church had to deal with change, too. Jesus originally directed his teachings to people in a Jewish culture. As the faith moved into new cultures, new questions were raised. A letter such as First Corinthians shows the problems of applying the gospel to a different cultural setting. Eating meat offered to idols was not a problem Jesus addressed (because the meat in Judea was butchered according to the law of Moses), but it was a real issue for those who lived in a city where most butcher shops were connected with local pagan temples that made the meats left over from the pagan sacrifices. In 1 Corinthians 8 and 10 Paul deals with these issues, trying to apply the basic beliefs of the church to this specific situation. In particular, Paul empha- sizes the main duty of Christians to love one another and to encourage each other in the faith as the guiding principle in the dispute (hence, allowing people to eat meat wherever it was sac- rificed, unless it caused others problems in their faith; see Rom. 14:1-15; 1 Cor. 8:9-13.) For Paul, the key was not eating meat, but what helped people believe in Christ.

John 16 anticipates the central problem of dealing with issues and situations that were not directly addressed in the earlier teachings of Jesus:

> I still have many things to say to you, but you cannot bear them now. When the Spirit of truth comes, he will guide you into all the truth; for he will not speak on his own, but will speak whatever he hears, and he will declare to you the things that are to come. He will glorify me, because he will take what is mine and declare it to you. All that the Father has is mine. For this reason I said that he will take what is mine and declare it to you (Jn. 16:12-15).

Jesus is warning the disciples that they have not heard from him everything they need to know. He could hardly anticipate every conceivable contingency for the future, warn them about it, and expect them to remember what he said when the time came.

Some things will have to be covered in the context of that mission and not before.

The role of the Holy Spirit in the future will be to lead the disciples into "all the truth." This suggests a dynamic understanding of revelation. Jesus is "the truth" (Jn. 14:6), but not simply as a static bundle of doctrine or propositions. The "truth" must always relate to Jesus (who he was and what his life and death meant), but new questions will arise in coming times that are not addressed explicitly in the specific sayings of Jesus. As the situation changes, the meaning of what we have learned in Christ must be reapplied and expressed again in order to become the fresh and timely revelation of God's salvation for that moment.

This sounds dangerous, and it is. Then again, *not* responding to changing situations has its own set of dangers. Is Jesus saying that truth is strictly relative and changes from situation to situation? No! In fact, some significant boundaries are set for the future guidance of the Holy Spirit in these verses. The Holy Spirit cannot act "on his own" (Jn. 16:13), but only as directed from above. Any "new" leading of the Spirit must be seen in continuity with the known teaching of Jesus.

We may be able to see this a bit better if we borrow a "working model" suggested by N. T. Wright:

> Suppose there exists a Shakespeare play, most of whose fifth act has been lost. The first four acts provide, let us suppose, such a remarkable wealth of characterization, such a crescendo of excitement within the plot, that it is felt inappropriate actually to write a fifth act once and for all: it would freeze the play into one form, and commit Shakespeare as it were to being prospectively responsible for work not in fact his own. Better, it might be felt to give the parts to highly trained, sensitive and experienced Shakespearian actors, who would immerse themselves in the first four acts, and in the language and culture of

Shakespeare and his time, and who would then be told to work out a fifth act for themselves (italics original).[10]

What Dr. Wright is applying to the act of interpreting scripture, we might also apply to the operation of the Holy Spirit implied in John 16. The Spirit is so imbued, connected, and consistent with the work and person of Jesus, that Spirit will act in persons of faith to lead them to apply the teachings and truth of Christ in new situations in a manner consistent with teachings and intentions of Jesus. It is, indeed, *his* Spirit.

How is the church to know whether a particular person is being guided by the Spirit of Truth or is an imposter? The key, according to John 16:14, lies in who gets the glory. The pseudo-spirit will speak for selfish gain or power. The Spirit of Truth will point people toward Christ and glorify him.

A David Koresh or a Jim Jones will claim spiritual inspiration for his words and deeds, but the real source of their "inspiration" seems clear to most people. These people used their claims to gain money and sexual favors from their followers, and to develop and maintain a position of control over their community. The willingness to destroy people for personal glory and satisfaction surely contradicts the Christ who died for others.

Jesus is suggesting that we must deliberately test new ideas and concepts against Christ's teachings and character. Our earlier reference to John Wesley detailed his own reluctance in trying Whitefield's "new" idea of field preaching. Wesley's approach to the question follows what John 16 implies. First, he looked to the biblical record. Could you find a link between biblical practice and belief? Second, Wesley evaluated the results of the innovation. Did people grow in their faith or fall away? Was the church built up or weakened? Was Christ honored or brought into disrepute? Only when Wesley satisfied himself that adequate biblical precedence for field preaching existed in the preaching ministry of Jesus, and that the results were consistent with

Christ's intentions, did he leave the comfort of the parish pulpit for the unknowns of the field and the marketplace.

Where the Holy Spirit is leading the church into change, people are brought into a deeper faith, a closer connection with the church, and a greater appreciation of Christ. Where the innovation reflects mostly the ego or power needs of individuals involved, the results tend to be conflict and chaos and the loss of people. These observations do not give us simple, hard and fast rules, but they do give us guidelines in applying the gospel to new and changing times.

Often the process of discerning the leadership of the Holy Spirit takes time. A pastor was assigned to a struggling, inner-city church. The average age of the remaining congregation was almost sixty-five. He felt that, for the congregation to survive, they had to find ways to invite and keep younger families. Developing worship that was exciting and meaningful for younger families seemed to him to be an absolute necessity. Over time, he worked with people in the church to bring newer and more contemporary music into the worship service. He tried to move slowly enough not to alienate older members, but some left anyway. Not everyone believed his leadership was led by the Holy Spirit. Over time, however, most of the older members stayed, and younger families began to come. Now this dying, inner-city church enjoys a worshiping congregation more than four times larger than before. Over time, the changes he felt led to introduce have been vindicated, but the process was slow and required constant testing and evaluation.

Finding the guidance of the Holy Spirit, focusing on glorifying Christ, and being faithful to our traditions is not an easy business in these contexts. Yet the failure to respond in Christ to new situations means that we miss the new opportunities that come with these situations. Jesus tells us that the leadership of the Spirit will be available to us. We must test the answer we find, but answers will be there.

Making It Through Change

The second half of John 16 begins by taking a saying from chapter 13 and reapplying it to the new situation. In John 13:33, Jesus told the disciples he would be with them just a "little longer" before leaving, anticipating his coming death on the cross. Now in John 16:16 Jesus takes this idea and reapplies it, "A little while, and you will no longer see me, and again a little while, and you will see me." The statement confuses the disciples who wonder, naturally, what are these two "little whiles."

In the immediate context of the Gospel story, the "little whiles" seem to refer to the period between the cross and the resurrection. For a while, the disciples will be plunged into deep despair, while their enemies rejoice. Then something will happen to turn it all around. The cross will bring a sense of pain and abandonment to the disciples. For a time it will seem as if Jesus has lost and his enemies have triumphed, but in the resurrection they will see that the cross in God's hands becomes the means to victory and joy.

From yet another angle, the two references to "a little while" imply something beyond the immediate experience of the disciples. Jesus ends the chapter with a general statement: "In the world you face persecution. But, take courage; I have conquered the world!" (Jn. 16:33). Troubles and difficulties are not limited to the days between Good Friday and Easter. The disciples will find that sorrow dogs many days. Still, Jesus always offers hope for joy at the end of sorrow. The resurrection happened not only in history—it happens over and over again in the individual lives of Christians before the final resurrection. Jesus has overcome the world, and, therefore, our individual sorrows will be overcome.

However, to enjoy this triumph over sorrow, the disciple must make it through the temptation to give up in despair. Jesus uses the image of a woman in labor in these verses (Jn. 16:20-22). As a male, I cannot claim to know exactly what he means. However, being of the generation that embraced "natural" childbirth and avoided drugs in labor and delivery, I did have the privilege of being with my wife through these experiences. For various reasons, labor, and especially delivery, were ordeals for her. I suffered enough just watching her, and I can only imagine how hard it was for her. There were points where she would have been tempted to back out if nature had allowed! It was all she could do to hang on and keep on using the birthing techniques we had learned. But at the end, all this was irrelevant. She did not forget the struggle, but she was so overjoyed with the child and convinced of the positive results of avoiding drugs, that the results seemed worth the cost.

Jesus is telling us that, at times, all we will be able to do will be to hang on. At that time the critical decision for us will be to continue to believe and to wait, knowing that the results will be worth it. We, too, can overcome the world, and indeed find the joy and peace of Jesus (Jn. 16:22, 32), but only by staying on the course and not giving up.

In our birthing classes, trainers worked with Sandi and me to teach us the breathing and mental techniques that would help her deal with the contractions in labor. We practiced them over and over in the days before delivery. During the birth of our first child, we found out that real labor was quite different from our simulated practices—we felt we had not prepared quite enough! But the techniques did help Sandi maintain a minimum of control.

In dealing with the trials and tribulations of life, Jesus again reminds us that we have something that will help us make it through those tough times—prayer. He reminds the disciples again that their prayers are heard (Jn. 16:23-24). Moreover, the disciples are urged to pray in these circumstances, not to him, but directly to the Father. Jesus is promising the disciples that the Father will be personally available to them in their need. They can pray in faith, needing no intermediary, believing that God is listening and responding to them. In the end, the disciples will receive joy, complete joy, that cannot be taken away from them.

The disciples (and through them, we) are being told that difficulties, opposition, and sorrows will occur in our lives. But eventually God overcomes and even uses these times to bring us joy. We should not be surprised when times get tough, nor should we feel intimidated. We are being encouraged to trust God's ability to take us through the hard times and to redeem them. Jesus in no way trivializes suffering, but in the cross he shows that the pain of suffering is not God's last word.

Sam Brengle, an early leader of the Salvation Army, was involved in street preaching in nineteenth-century London. In those days the Army often aroused fierce opposition and even hostility for their unusual ministry. One day, during a service on the street, a brick was thrown from out of the crowd that hit Brengle, knocking him unconscious and putting him in the hospital. For a long time, Brengle hovered near death and finally began a slow recovery. He was forced to spend long months rehabilitating in bed. During that time, he fought depression by beginning to write a book on prayer which was later published and wildly successful. Many people found Brengle's work personally helpful. Later, when sympathetic friends would speak with regret of the incident that put him in the hospital, Brengle would reply, "Without the brick, there would have been no book." His suffering was real, but God had redeemed it to the point that he no longer regretted the incident that caused such pain.

Of course, it is much easier to talk about suffering than to go through it! Especially during the season of Lent, we contemplate the sufferings of Christ for us. We dedicate ourselves to the call of Christ and commit ourselves to solidarity with Christ and the cross. Yet can we really know what this means? Chapter 16 ends with a highly ironic conversation between Jesus and the disciples. He asks them if they understand what he is saying, and they respond confidently that they understand completely. But they do not. Within hours they will be scattered by the events following the supper and confused by the betrayal and death of their Lord. They do not yet understand what suffering really means, and they will not know until they go through it.

We can discuss suffering in the abstract, but personally growing through pain and sorrow will be completely different. As a pastor, I am continually amazed at the faith and courage of people with whom I minister. One Sunday, while preaching on suffering and faith, I looked out and saw a particular parishioner. Knowing her story, I hesitated in the midst of my sermon. I knew that she had experienced far more concretely the topic of my sermon than I had. Frankly, preaching to her on suffering was intimidating. Her husband had left her with four children and no money. She had struggled through the divorce, keeping the family together, and finally met and remarried another man. The marriage went well, but within months her second husband fell ill and finally died from cancer. From the two marriages, she now had six children for whom she was caring. Yet as I preached on God's goodness in the midst of suffering, she sat beaming back at me, nodding her head in agreement.

I could not know the depth of the truth that Christ offers joy after sorrow as she did. But she gave me faith to go on, because I could see the joy in her face despite all that she had been through. Looking at the disciples, Jesus knew that they did not understand what he meant, but that they would learn. And in the end they would come to trust his words, "In the world you face persecution. But take courage; I have conquered the world!" (Jn. 16:33).

◼ *Discussion Questions*

1. Do you think the Holy Spirit calls us to challenge some religious authorities today? Give some examples and discuss.

2. What is it about innovation or change that threatens people? Tell about an experience of change you have gone through, and how your faith has helped you to understand, even to embrace it.

3. The key to evaluating the leading of the Holy Spirit according to John 16 is that the Holy Spirit will glorify Christ. Give some examples of situations today where you think this key is crucial in evaluating the guidance of the Spirit.

4. What is the problem with asserting that God will change the sorrow of the faithful into joy? What help does Jesus give us in this chapter?

6
SET APART AND SENT IN

I remember clearly when he came in. He met with the pastors and his lawyer to tell us about a great project that was just about to bear fruit. When the deal was closed, he was proposing to give the church his tithe to help start our building project. He expected a great deal of money, and he made us all excited about the prospects.

To be truthful, however, we hedged our excitement a bit. We did not know this man well, and we knew enough about business to be wary of counting on contracts before they were signed. It was well that we did not get too carried away, for the contract never happened, the man disappeared, and the building waited several more years to get started.

Contrast this with the story Maxie Dunnam tells about Lewis Department Store in Birmingham, England. The Lewis store was large and prosperous and hoping to expand their store to meet a rising demand in business. The lot next to their store was occupied by a small Friends' meetinghouse. The Lewis management wrote to the Society of Friends, offering to meet their price and buy the lot. They received a note in return which read something like this:

> Dear Sir,
> We note your desire to extend your store and that our property is in the way. However, we have been here longer than you. So, if you will name a suitable price, we will buy Lewis.
>
> CADBURY

The Cadbury family, of course, were the wealthy owners of the famous English candy manufacturer and faithful members of that Society of Friends meetinghouse. And, as Dr. Dunnam concluded, "It's not how big the building is, but who signs the letter" that counts. Unlike the man who talked with us, the Cadbury family had the resources and ability to follow through and to make their offer happen.

At the end of a "Farewell Discourse," the main speaker often prays for his family and followers, asking God's blessing on them and praying for their future. John 17 gives us Jesus' final prayer for the disciples. In it, Jesus prays for his disciples, commissioning them to their ministry, seeking God's protection and care for them. We know this prayer will come true, because it is *Jesus* who is praying. As we complete our study, John 17 gives us a chance to review again the call of Christ on our lives, and our response to his gift of himself.

The Prayer of the Faithful Son

In verses that remind us of John 13:31-32, John 17 begins with Jesus petitioning the Father to "glorify" him as he ends his work on earth. As in John 13, the petition for glory does not reflect any selfish desire for honor on Jesus' part. Rather, these verses look forward to the cross and resurrection as the final act of God's reaching out through the Son to save the world. The "glory" that Jesus seeks will come in the resurrection. Easter will vindicate Jesus as God's servant, and God as Jesus' loving Father for the whole world to see.

The beginning of John 17 does more than ask the Father to fulfill the final part of the divine plan, however. These verses form the basis for the petitions in the rest of the prayer. In these verses, Jesus claims that he has acted as the commissioned agent of the Father (Jn. 17:2), bringing life to those who belong to God. Jesus left his heavenly position to serve God (Jn. 17:5).

Having completed his work on earth (Jn. 17:4), he is ready to return to his former position of heavenly glory. Christ has been faithful. Now God must show the world who the Son really is through responding to his prayer.

All petitions in prayer have some "basis" or reason for asking God to act. Often we petition God on the basis of God's mercy or love or on the basis of the covenant God has made with faithful people. Here Jesus petitions God on the basis of God's plan in sending the Son to the world, and on the basis of his own faithfulness.

Needless to say, this is not something many of us would feel comfortable doing. But Christ *was* faithful and *did fulfill* his commission, and therefore has the right to petition God in this way.

Ultimately, these verses base the future of the church on the faithfulness of Christ. In this sense, our relationship with God depends not so much on our performance, but on what the Son has done for us. This does not mean that disciples have no responsibilities on their side. Still less is Jesus saying that we can do what we want without any demands being put on us by God. However, Jesus did the real work for us. The faithfulness of Christ is complete (Jn. 17:4). The conditions have been met, and our relationship with God is built on this sure foundation.

In the cross and the resurrection we recognize what has always been true: Christ came from God to us and for us, and now has returned to the glory he always had. Our future is based upon this wonder. We can have confidence, because Jesus has done his work for us and done it well.

In the midst of anxiety, frustration, and failure, we do well to remember that Christ's work for us gives us the basis for our future. Our failures may be real and significant, but we can always go back to the fact of Jesus' life for us. The prayers of Christ for us still offer hope and consolation.

People of the Name

In John 17:6, Jesus makes an intriguing claim: "I have made your name known to those whom you gave me from the world." What does this mean? It may help to compare this with further descriptions of the disciples in the next few verses:

"they have kept your word" (Jn. 17:6b)

"Now they know that everything you have given me is from you" (Jn. 17:7)

"the words that you gave to me, I have given to them, and they have received them and know in truth that I came from you" (Jn. 17:8)

"they have believed that you sent me" (Jn.17:8d)

Jesus states that he has revealed the Father's "name" to the disciples, given them the "word" (*logos*) given to him, and the "words" (*ramata*) given to him. The disciples have "kept," "received," "known," and "believed" these various revelations.

To know the name of God is to know the character of God. In magical rites of Jesus' day, superstitious believers thought that by using the name of a deity they could make the deity answer their prayers. Only the most intimate and significant believers in a religion were given the name of the deity. The name implied special power and privilege.

In John 17, to know the name of God means to believe in Jesus, in his words, and in his mission for the Father. The disciples are those who have accepted the claims of Christ and trust him. They have believed, as Peter said in John 6:68, that he alone has the "words of eternal life." They are the ones who have staked their futures on the faithfulness of Christ.

Therefore, Jesus prays for the disciples here, because they have accepted his teachings and revelation. This shows that these people really belong to God. They have not responded completely on their own initiative, but as part of God's plan. These are God's people, and Jesus has taken care of them for the Father.

These verses suggest that the people of God are principally defined through their trust in God. Our faithfulness to the message and witness of Christ is what makes us true disciples. Those who receive, believe, and trust in the word of God revealed in Christ are marked and set apart.

Even in our smallish community, we see a stream of people coming through our church every day. They want help and expect the church to help them. We do as much as we can (not always enough), but the fascinating thing is how people expect us to be different. They walk past dozens of institutions to the church, feeling the church will surely help.

Receiving the revelation of God through Christ goes beyond intellectual assent. We literally become different people. We take on some of the character of God (which is why people expect generosity and help from us). Unlike the superstitious folk of Jesus' time, the disciples learn that knowing the "name" of God does not give them special power over God. Rather, our confession of faith in Christ means that we come under special obligation to God. Knowing the "name" of God claims us for God, not God for us.

At the same time, of course, because we belong to the Father, God does have special care and concern for us. The intention in these verses is to set aside the disciples to carry on the ministry of Christ. To do that, they will need the special care and protection of the Father. Becoming people of the name, the disciples will represent the will of the Father for the world, and they will need the ongoing presence of God in all that they do.

Left In

In the middle section of the prayer (Jn. 17:9-15), Jesus prays fervently for the future of the disciples. The petitions here envisage the disciples in the middle of a hostile, questioning world. The disciples will be "in the world" (Jn. 17:11), but not of the world (Jn. 17:14). Because they represent Jesus and remain faithful to the word he has given them, they will experience the hatred of the world (Jn. 17:14). All the opposition directed toward Jesus will be redirected toward his followers once he leaves.

The prayer actually pictures the situation of the disciples from the other side of Easter ("I am no longer in the world," Jn. 17:11). The cross and resurrection, though chronologically ahead in the story, are taken as accomplished deeds. From now on, the disciples will not have the protection of Jesus as they did during his life (Jn. 17:12), and the key petition of this section comes in verse 11: "Holy Father, protect them in your name that you have given me, so that they may be one, as we are one." Jesus fears that the pressure of opposition might tear the young church apart. Therefore, he prays that the disciples will remain true to their faith and witness once he leaves this world, and that they will remain unified in that witness.

After Jesus' death, the disciples did face real and powerful forces. At times they were attacked for their faith and persecuted (refer to Stephen in Acts 6). They must have been tempted to give up and to split up. Only their common commitment to Christ kept the young church true to the message Jesus had given them.

Most North American churches face more danger from internal conflict than from external persecution, but the end result can look very similar to problems Jesus anticipated for the disciples. When conflict hits a church, people tend to split into groups, cutting off communication with each other. The emphasis switches from the message of Christ to the personalities and issues involved in the dispute. The witness of the church is undermined.

A group of three of us went visiting four very different churches to study their special strengths. Two were older churches and two were new church plants. Two were United Methodist and two were not. The four churches were located in Minnesota, California, and Alabama.

I thought the four would be quite different due to their unique histories and locations. But with all their differences, they were remarkably similar. All four showed a remarkable lack of internal dissension, although they had gone through a good deal of change. I noticed that my "established" churches had this in common with the new church plants: They had changed sites in fairly recent history. They did so to reach new people for Christ more effectively. We found this common thread among the four churches: Each had a definite commitment to reaching people outside of themselves. It seemed to me that the lack of dissension and the focus on others went together.

Healthy churches overcome their differences through a commitment to what matters—their witness to Christ. If the church remains focused on the goal of lifting up Christ, lesser distractions and arguments tend to be just that—lesser. As one Southern preacher put it, "You can't row the boat and rock the boat at the same time." What protects the church from both external and internal pressures will be the common devotion of disciples to the message of Christ for others.

Significantly, Jesus stresses that the pressure on the disciples will not give them an excuse to flee the "world." A normal human response to conflict and pressure is to run away! But Jesus assumes that the disciples will and must remain "in the world." Because, even with the hatred of the world, the mission of the church remains the same as the mission of Jesus—to reach out to a hurting and rebellious world that God still loves (Jn. 3:16-17).

The disciples had to face both the opposition of the world and the temptation to resolve the crisis of opposition through separating from the world. They could have stayed together and stayed in their faith, while avoiding the conflict implicit in witness by avoiding those who might disagree with them. However, Jesus explicitly rejected this idea. They would be in the world. They would experience conflict. What would keep them safe in the midst of this was not running and hiding, but being faithful to the message of Christ.

Churches, too, are tempted with the comfort of becoming islands of faith separate from the rest of humanity. Too often, our circle of friends includes only other Christians who share our basic faith and values, and with whom we have only trivial disagreements. Outside of the narrow band of people with whom we already agree, we rarely interact on a faith level. We may do business with other people, and even talk with them, but we leave faith matters out of our conversation.

To be people who have truly accepted the words and revelation that Jesus offers, we cannot keep our faith to ourselves. Sharing what we believe and who we are is dangerous. Those who do so often find opposition from some source. But Jesus expects the disciples to serve and share as he has served, and he prays for their protection and their courage in facing the opposition that comes with faith.

Set Apart and Sent In

In John 17:17 Jesus prays, "Sanctify them in the truth; your word is truth." Something sanctified is set apart for use in God's service. The word *sanctify* in Greek comes from the same root as the word we translate "holy." However, something sanctified is not in and of itself "holy" in character. The temple vessels and tools were "sanctified" for use in the sacrificial system. The use of the vessel in the worship of God lends holiness to the utensil, not the other way around.

The disciples similarly find their holiness in their mission. They are sanctified "in the truth." Truth, here, does not suggest philosophical or scientific truth. Jesus has already proclaimed himself as "the way, and the truth, and the life" in John 14:6. In John 4:23, Jesus promised the Samaritan woman that true worshipers would soon worship "in spirit and truth" and not in a place such as the temple. Indeed, after the resurrection, the disciple Thomas will fall before the risen Jesus and declare, "My Lord and my God!" (Jn. 20:28). Jesus proclaims and embodies the truth. True worship is worship of Jesus. It is this faith and this worship that will sanctify and set apart the disciples from the world.

Certainly there are other truths in the world. The church has no monopoly on scientific, political, or economic truths. We do not even have a monopoly on kindness and love. We can and should acknowledge the justice and righteousness in the actions of others and join with them to promote good for those in need.

However, we do have this truth: God has come in Jesus Christ in a real and final way for our lives and for the lives of all who will believe. This truth sets us apart and makes the church different from other organizations.

From this we also receive our mission. Jesus states in John 17:18, "As you have sent me into the world, so I have sent them into the world. And for their sakes I sanctify myself, so that they also may be sanctified in truth." The mission of Jesus is given over to the disciples, and through them to us. Christ accepted the call of the Father to go into the world to save people, and he calls the disciples to carry on that mission.

Looking back over church history, we see how easily the church can lose its distinctive character. When Christians have become tied up with nationalism, the church has been little more than an extension of the state. Sometimes modern American Christianity appears to be more of an extension of American consumerism than a reflection of the truth of Christ.

Each culture has a tendency to remake Christ in its own image. Around the turn of the century, Albert Schweitzer analyzed the "life of Jesus" studies done in liberal Protestant circles. He discovered that almost inevitably these studies rendered a Jesus who talked and acted like a good, liberal German Protestant.[11] Lately, people have noticed a "blending of the religious and the psychological" in many popular Christian works.[12] In these days of the ascendance of psychology, we often find Jesus portrayed as a help to self-esteem and self-actualization. At its extreme, some preaching and some literature come close to making Jesus into a "self-help savior" offering affirmation and encouragement to the alienated society.

When Christians turn away from Christ as our real center, we tend to look like pale imitations of whatever we are copying. Christian nationalists tend to look like a more polite version of undiluted nationalism. Christian psychology tends to look like a more spiritualized and less self-absorbed version of secular psychology.

The one constant in all of this remains Jesus himself. Despite the pressure to make Jesus conform to our culture, he continues to call people to himself, breaking down cultural and national barriers, transcending our temporal limitations. But in devotion to Christ, and in seeking to follow him, the church separates itself from the popular culture and becomes something different and unique.

I have had the opportunity to meet and hear missionary Bruce Olson a number of times. His story would fill a book, but to put it briefly, as a young man he felt called to go to the jungles of Colombia to seek out the warlike Montilone tribe. He made contact with them and shared with them the good news about Jesus. Assuming that God had made the Montilone culture, he worked hard not to impose Western culture on them. But seeing they were hungry, he did help them develop cooperative farms. The primitive state of the Montilones left them very vulnerable to disease, so he helped open clinics and got training for Montilone nurses to care for their own sick. That required opening schools to enable young Montilones to get training, and finally opening negotiations with the federal government to ensure Montilone land and rights.

Through all this, Olson tried to make the Montilones master of their own fate. He refused official positions and trained the Montilones to take over their own economic cooperatives, schools, and clinics as soon as possible. The progress of the Montilones was watched with concern by Marxist guerrillas in the area, and they finally decided to kidnap Olson so that the system he had set up would collapse. They truly believed that only a Marxist-socialist system would help the desperately poor people of their region. They felt sure that Montilone success was a deception, a mirage that would disappear as soon as Olson was taken out.

They did kidnap him, but to their surprise, the Montilones continued as before. What the Montilones had created (Bruce would disclaim authorship of much of what happened) was neither socialist nor capitalist. What they had created flowed out of their reverence for Christ. How long and how well the Montilones will succeed remains to be seen. But Olson's commitment to Christ led him to try to treat the Montilones and their culture with respect and to avoid "Westernizing" them as he shared the good news with them. As a result, the Montilones did not depend on Olson and went on doing well during his captivity (which finally ended when the guerrillas safely returned him).

I am sure that the Montilones and Bruce Olson have their own weaknesses; but to the extent that they are faithful to Christ, this has set them apart from the world. To be "wholly" Christ's sanctifies us and equips us to carry on the mission of Christ. The pressure to combine "our gospel" with the truth of Christ exists for all of us, but it is the truth of Christ that truly defines us and our mission.

Through Them to Us

In John 17:20, Jesus extends the intent of the prayer past the original set of disciples to include us: "I ask, not only on behalf of these, but also on behalf of those who will believe in me through their word." His prayer for us is not only that we believe through the witness of these disciples, but that those who believe will share the unity that Jesus and the Father enjoy (Jn. 17:21, 23).

These verses have often been lifted up by the ecumenical movement as a battle cry. Unity among Christians surely does represent a goal in this prayer. A disunified church will not convince the world of the truth of Christ. Non-Christians are often bewildered by the amazing plurality of denominations in Christianity. To them it argues against what we proclaim. How can Jesus be the resurrected Lord if his followers are so fractious and unloving toward each other?

However, ecumenism should not exaggerate the stress on structural unity in these verses. The oneness of the disciples with each other parallels the oneness of Christ with the Father. The Son and the Father have a unity of will and mission, which is to proclaim life through the Son. Unity among believers comes when we likewise join together in a common witness to Christ.

A common commitment to communicate our love of Christ and God can overshadow organizational distinctions. Billy Graham's crusades have often brought together diverse parts of the Christian community in a powerful show of unity built around the desire to reach out to people who do not know Christ. Similarly, people in the modern charismatic movement have found the ability to reach across denominational and racial lines in dramatic fashion, celebrating their common faith and experience in Christ.

In my college years we had two main Christian groups on campus: the Chapel Fellowship and the Evangelical Fellowship.

The nonstudent leadership of the latter strongly rejected any sense of cooperation with outside groups. However, some of us felt that it was important for the witness on campus to try to show that we had more in common than our difference. I knew that we needed to do something. I had talked with some friends, and they had bluntly told me, "If you Christians can't even get along here, why should we take Jesus seriously?" A group of us decided to live together on campus. We did not want to create a new group, and we honored our differences of opinion. We tried to show by our actions that our common faith in Christ was real, even if we still disagreed over the details.

During the time the two groups lived together, not everything went smoothly. But the number of people attending the functions of both the Chapel Fellowship and the Evangelical Fellowship more than doubled during the year. I will always believe that our decision to live together and our increased ability to influence people were connected. To my recollection, none of us in the Chapel Fellowship ever convinced our friends in the Evangelical Fellowship that we were right and they were wrong—but somehow our love for one another came through our disagreements.

In the final verse of the prayer Jesus says, "I made your name known to them, and I will make it known, so that the love with which you have loved me may be in them, and I in them" (Jn. 17:26). When the love of God dwells in the people of God, then Jesus' prayer for us has truly been answered. This love is never mushy or sentimental. The love of God was most perfectly reflected in the cross of Christ. When Christians sacrifice themselves in the service of Christ and of other people, then that love continues to live on in the church.

The church by no means perfectly reflects the love that Jesus prays for. Individual and institutional selfishness often binds us. But amazingly, God still works through us. With all our foibles and weaknesses, we are still protected from falling utterly into evil. The witness to Christ is still handed on, generation to generation. As many mistakes as we make, the mission of Christ goes on through us. Through individual Christians and churches, the love of God is expressed truly and powerfully, so that people do believe in Christ through our words. The prayer of Jesus seems even now to be effective for us.

Christ calls us to become wholly his and to go into the world for his sake. In the midst of this, if we are honest, we will admit that not only are we truly "in the world," but at times it appears that more than a little bit of the world is in us. Our witness creates a tension not only between us and those who do not believe, but also within ourselves. Our comfort is not in our personal performance, but the Christ who has perfectly fulfilled his commission has prayed for us to fulfill ours. As we are faithful to Christ, we are truly set apart to carry on the mission of Christ. And as often and as far as that happens, people continue to be drawn to the message and to the life offered in Christ.

◙ *Discussion Questions*

1. John 17 contemplates the return of Jesus to his former place of "glory" with the Father (Jn. 17:4, 5, 25). How does the triumph of Christ give you hope for your future?

2. If the genuine holiness of the church is to be found in its mission beyond the church building, where are the places of holiness and mission for you and for your congregation?

3. What do you believe are the key obstacles to unity among Christians? Have you ever seen these obstacles overcome? (If possible, give examples.)

4. To be people of "the Name" means that we are actually being formed in the very way we live our lives. Discuss some of the places in your life where you sense God may be at work, and offer prayers of encouragement for one another.

◼ Notes

[1]Robert E. Stevens, David L. Loudon, and R. Wade Paschal, Jr., "A Survey of Pastors' Continuing Education Needs in Leadership and Management Skills," *Journal of Ministry and Management* (January 1994).

[2]Bernard Shaw, *Complete Plays with Prefaces*, Vol. I (New York: Dodd, Mead & Company, 1962), pp. 229-30.

[3]This story is found in Ernest Gordon, *Through the Valley of the Kwai* (New York: Harper and Row, Publishers, 1962), pp. 104-05.

[4]The text is from Richard P. Heitzenrater, *The Elusive Mr. Wesley: John Wesley His Own Biographer*, Vol. I (Nashville: Abingdon Press, 1984), p. 199.

[5]Lance Webb, *The Art of Personal Prayer* (Nashville: Abingdon, 1977), pp. 61f.

[6]Thomas R. Albin, *Full Salvation: The Spirituality of Anna Reynalds of Truro, 1775-1840* (Cornish Methodist Historical Association, Occasional Publication No. 17, 1981), p. 19. The quote is from Anna's personal journal.

[7]Ken C. Kinghorn, *Fresh Wind of the Spirit* (Nashville: Abingdon Press, 1975), p. 84.

[8]Heitzenrater, *The Elusive Mr. Wesley*, p. 107.

[9]Ibid., p. 128.

[10]N. T. Wright, *The New Testament and the People of God*, Vol. I (Minneapolis: Fortress Press, 1992), p. 140.

[11]Albert Schweitzer, *The Quest for the Historical Jesus*, trans. by W. Montgomery (New York: Macmillan, 1961).

[12]Wade Clark Roof, *A Generation of Seekers: The Spiritual Journeys of the Baby Boom Generation* (New York: Harper Collins Publishers, 1993), p. 71.